Thomas Cook

TRAVELLERS

VANCOUVER &
BRITISH COLUMBIA

By
CAROL BAKER

Written by Carol Baker, updated by Pam Mandel
Original photography by Helena Zukowski

Published by Thomas Cook Publishing
A division of Thomas Cook Tour Operations Limited.
Company registration no. 1450464 England
The Thomas Cook Business Park, 9 Coningsby Road,
Peterborough PE3 8SB, United Kingdom
E-mail: books@thomascook.com, Tel: + 44 (0) 1733 416477
www.thomascookpublishing.com

Produced by Cambridge Publishing Management Limited
Burr Elm Court, Main Street, Caldecote CB23 7NU

ISBN: 978-1-84157-930-6

© 2002, 2006 Thomas Cook Publishing
This third edition © 2008
Text © Thomas Cook Publishing
Maps © Thomas Cook Publishing

Series Editor: Linda Bass
Production/DTP: Steven Collins

Printed and bound in Italy by Printer Trento

Cover photography: Front L–R: © World Pictures/Photoshot;
© Chris Anderson/Getty Images/Aurora Creative.
Back L–R: © dk/Alamy; © f1 online/Alamy.

The paper used for this book has been independently certified as having
been sourced from well-managed forests and recycled wood or fibre
according to the rules of the Forest Stewardship Council.
This book has been printed and bound in Italy by Printer Trento S.r.l.,
an FSC certified company for printing books on FSC mixed paper in
compliance with the chain of custody and on products labelling standards.

FSC
Mixed Sources
Product group from well-managed
forests and recycled wood or fibre

Cert no. CQ-COC-000012
www.fsc.org
© 1996 Forest Stewardship Council

Contents

KEY TO MAPS

✈ Airport

🚗⑨⑨Ⓐ Road number

3954m ▲ Mountain

• • Ferry route

⭐ Start of walk/tour

● SkyTrain Station

Introduction

British Columbia, often referred to as BC, joined the Canadian Confederation in 1871, but is still regarded as a youngster in the world community. The life of this 'youngster', however, extends a long way back in time, to the creation of the majestic Coast Mountains, 130 million years ago. The north, with its extremes of temperature, is sparsely populated, while the urban centres of Vancouver and Victoria, where the climate is kind, are attracting more and more people all the time.

The first residents were Asian hunters and berry gatherers, who drifted south along the coast and into the interior around 6000 BC. The first visitor to arrive by sea was probably Hoei-Shin, a Chinese Buddhist priest who sailed across the Pacific in AD 499.

Although the Spanish explorer Balboa claimed the Pacific Ocean and

Jogging at Coal Harbour

all its shores for Spain in 1513, the Spaniards did not settle here until the late 18th century. They stayed only a few years, but left their names: Cardero, Valdez, Juan de Fuca, Bodega y Quadra and Malaspina. Explorations by adventurers such as Captain Cook, Alexander Mackenzie, George Vancouver and Simon Fraser resulted in an influx of British settlers, and the area became a British colony in 1858.

Today, ironically, the Asians are back. More than 150,000 Chinese Canadians now live in BC. Other Chinese, both from Hong Kong and Taiwan, are investing in business, property and a new way of life in large numbers. The Japanese, who already own and manage many businesses in BC, also come by the jet-load on holidays, to marvel at the space, the wilderness, the native culture, and the slopes in Whistler, which they rate among the finest ski resorts of the world.

Vancouver, Canada's gateway to the Pacific, has become a wonderfully

BC's wild Pacific coast

cosmopolitan centre, often blending the best of both European and Asian ways of life and, at the same time, encouraging a rebirth of BC's native Indian cultures.

'There's wine in the cup, Vancouver, And there's warmth in my heart for you.'
Indian poetess Pauline Johnson, 1911

'Vancouver is one of those cities, like San Francisco, which are victims of their glorious settings. One expects too much of them. As Californians like to say, there is less to them than meets the eye.'
Travel writer Jan Morris, 1990

'I would not give the bleakest knoll on the bleakest hill of Scotland, for all these mountains in a heap.'
Explorer Captain John Gordon, 1844

'The history of Canada for about 300 years was a struggle to escape from the wilderness, and for the last half century has been a desperate attempt to escape into it.'
Canadian author Bruce Hutchison, 1953

'Every single time, when I come back to BC after a trip abroad, I thank my lucky stars I had the common sense to move here early enough in my life to truly appreciate the great natural beauty this province has to offer.'
Merchant banker Peter Thomas, 1991

'If I had known what it was like, I wouldn't have been content with a mere visit. I'd have been born here.'
Canadian humorist Stephen Leacock, 1937

Land and people

The BC motto, Splendor Sine Occasu, *which means 'splendour undiminished', is almost an understatement. Canada's most westerly province comprises 950,000sq km (366,797sq miles) of remarkably diverse seascapes and landforms – solitary beaches, quiet coves, primeval rainforests, spectacular fiords, snowcapped ranges, tundra, alpine meadows, glacial lakes, pristine waterfalls, rivers raging, and gentle, thermal springs, verdant valleys, plains and deserts.*

Geological past

About 130 million years ago, a gigantic upheaval in the earth's crust created the majestic Coast Mountains, the beginning of present-day BC. Sixty-five million years ago, further movements brought forth the Rocky Mountains, and 40 million years later, Cascadia, the Atlantis of the Pacific, sank offshore, leaving Vancouver Island and the Queen Charlotte Islands above sea level. A mere million years ago, most of BC was covered with a blanket of ice 2,500m (8,202ft) thick, which slowly began to recede 70,000 years later.

At one time, a thick layer of ice pressed down over the region; its retreat about 10,000 years ago left the vast and visually delightful panorama of mountains, canyons, fiords, rivers and swamps. Without the weight of the ice, the land lifted, and layers of marine shells have been found several hundred metres above sea level.

All Fraser River delta land west of New Westminster developed after the ice retreated, and alluvial soils continue to create several metres of new real estate here every year.

A century ago, workers extending Granville Street unearthed ancient tools, weapons and ornaments in the Marpole Midden, the largest of its kind discovered in North America to that date. A similar midden in Stanley Park

An early BC resident, Royal BC Museum, Victoria

provided so many seashells, emptied and discarded by hungry native First Nations residents, that park roads were once paved with them.

Vancouverites received a reminder that the earth is alive in 1980, when Mount St Helens in Washington erupted and spewed a film of fine ash over the city. One of Vancouver's most famous landmarks, Siwash Rock in Stanley Park, is the uneroded remnant of a small volcano within the city limits, and black volcanic rock underpins nearby Prospect Point. Volcanic rock was quarried for road material out of the city highpoint that today is Queen Elizabeth Park. Mount Garibaldi, a short drive east, was an active volcano 1,000 years ago. Constant landslides onto mountain roads are a regular reminder that geological processes work without pause.

Vancouver has even had several minor earthquakes. One in 1946 registered 7.3 on the Richter scale at the epicentre, which was fortunately some distance north. But buildings rocked, and the big clock on the Vancouver Block stopped. Seismologists say Vancouver and its environs are very likely to feel the impact of 'The Big One', if and when it comes, although everyone prays that it won't.

BC – the ultimate temperate rainforest

Natural features

Each day, the sun sets over 6,500 islands, offshore from a rugged 12,000km (7,458-mile) coastline indented by deep inlets. The magnificent Coast Mountains tower rank after rank in a northwest to southeast alignment. Eastward, a broad plateau of rolling rangeland, mantled with moraines and other glacial deposits, stretches towards the thrusting snowy peaks of the Rocky Mountains. These form a natural barrier between BC and the rest of Canada, which is accessible by land via mountain passes at Crowsnest, Kicking Horse and Yellowhead. Kimberly, located at an altitude of 1,100m (3,609ft), is the highest city in the country. North of the Rockies stretch the extensive fertile farmlands of the Peace River, a geographical continuation of the prairies.

The Fraser, Skeena, Nass, Stikine, Peace and Columbia rivers weave a web of routes and barriers throughout the province. The earth varies from the silty soil of the Fraser delta and the Okanagan Valley to the barren, lichen-covered lava fields of Terrace. Subterranean volcanic activity produces thermal springs at Harrison, Khalycon, Radium and Fairmont, which are open to the public for warm mineral baths.

Precipitation varies with topography, from the permanently damp rainforests of the Queen Charlotte Islands and frequent snowfalls of Mount Robson, the highest peak in the Rockies, to the sunny, arid Osoyoos desert with its cactuses, tumbleweed, sagebrush, lizards and rattlesnakes.

Taming the wilderness

Despite BC's vast and varied geography, man has made most areas accessible. A network of paved highways and railway tracks covers the countryside. The BC ferry fleet, the largest in the world, serves the islands and coastal towns, while in summer, luxury liners cruise to and from Alaska along the Inside Passage. International airports at Vancouver and Victoria, 350 other airfields and landing strips, and 100 seaplane bases permit access to remote regions.

Forestry and allied industries, which employ 80,000 British Columbians, face stiff pressure from increasing world competition which is eroding their traditional markets. Environmentalists, concerned over the future of the forests, are alarmed at how the forests are being managed.

Although timber, mining, agriculture and fishing all contribute to provincial coffers, tourism brings in the most revenue. Visitors, who are mostly other Canadians, Americans and Japanese, usually stay longer in BC than anywhere else in the country.

What nature has created, mankind has complemented with almost every conceivable recreational facility, resulting in a remarkable playground, especially in summer. More than 300 land parks and 32 marine parks offer wilderness varying from the 30 alpine lakes and five glaciers of Kokanee Glacier Provincial Park to the colourful underwater world of anemones, abalone and other aquatic creatures sought out by scuba divers along the coast.

Weather

If grey skies and wet weather bother you, it is better to gamble on the drier and sunnier summer. From November to March, it is often dark and rainy. About 250mm (10in) of rain drenches Vancouver in December, compared with 50mm (2in) in July. The thermometer hovers around 24°C (75°F) in July and around 6°C (43°F)

A mosaic of cultures in Vancouver

in December. Vancouver snows tend to be light and melt quickly. Winter rain downtown often means snow on the nearby mountains, so skiers can ski all day and evening and still get back downtown for a nightcap. Cool Pacific breezes make seashore strolls pleasant in summer. Now that wood and coal no longer heat homes, there is less smog than there used to be, but an occasional patch of fog can slow drivers down in autumn. Although a less drastic version of Los Angeles smog lays a thin beige blanket over the city, most visitors find the air refreshing.

The climate is kind in Victoria and Vancouver. Resources are abundant. Yet most of the wilderness remains wilderness.

The people

BC is a complexity of cultures. There has been an increasing variety of people coming to live in Vancouver during the past few decades, and the resulting mixture is exhilarating. Immigrants from Hong Kong, Taiwan, Japan, Vietnam and the Philippines in Asia, from Ethiopia, South Africa and Nigeria in Africa, from the USA, from many countries in Europe, and from Australasia have transformed the city. Everywhere, little neighbourhoods with a concentration of people from one culture keep popping up, and most of the world is represented in the restaurants offering international cuisine, and the shops selling souvenirs and objets d'art.

History

13 June 1792 Captain George Vancouver, exploring the Pacific Coast of North America, enters a body of water he names Burrard's Channel. Today, known as Burrard Inlet, it is the busy Vancouver harbour.

2 July 1808 Simon Fraser, seeking fur-trading routes, arrives at Musqueam at the mouth of the Fraser River, where the native people chase him and his men back upstream.

1846 After a long territorial dispute, a treaty is signed by Britain and the USA, placing BC firmly in Canada.

2 August 1858 Following the discovery of gold on the Fraser River, American miners begin to pour in. The British Parliament passes an act establishing the mainland colony of BC. The colony of Vancouver Island already exists.

25 November 1858 Colonel Richard Moody arrives with a company of 'sappers' (soldier engineers) and begins building roads. The first road built still exists, as North Road, now the boundary between the Vancouver suburbs of Burnaby and Coquitlam.

26 September 1862 The McCleery family become the first settlers in Vancouver when they occupy land on the north bank of the Fraser River on what is now McCleery Golf Course.

October 1862 Three new arrivals from England, John Morton, Samuel Brighouse and William Hailstone, file a claim on 202 hectares (500 acres) on Burrard Inlet. The land is empty, swampy forest, so other colonists laughingly call them 'The Three Greenhorns'. Today, that land, the city's apartment-crammed West End, is worth billions.

June 1863 A sawmill, the first industry in the area, is established on the north shore of Burrard Inlet.

30 September 1867	'Gassy' Jack Deighton, so nicknamed because he talked incessantly, builds a saloon in 24 hours with the help of thirsty sawmill workers. The area around his saloon becomes known as Gastown.
1869–70	Gastown gets a jail . . . and the name Granville.
20 July 1871	BC joins the Confederation of Canada, formed in 1867.
6 April 1886	The City of Vancouver, renamed from Granville, is incorporated.
13 June 1886	The Great Fire destroys most buildings in the new little city, and 20 people die. Rebuilding begins at once.
23 May 1887	The first Canadian Pacific Railway (CPR) passenger train arrives in Vancouver; Vancouver's growth begins to accelerate.
1902	Vancouver's population reaches 30,000. Charles Woodward opens Vancouver's first department store.
1904	The Great Northern Railway reaches Vancouver.
1908	The University of BC is founded, which today has 30,000 students.
1913	The World Building is completed, the tallest in the British Empire at the time. Today, known as the Old Sun Tower, it looks rather modest.
28 August 1915	The first Canadian Northern Pacific Railway train arrives in Vancouver. Later, the line becomes known as the Canadian National Railway (CNR).
1 November 1919	The CNR Station opens. Today it is the terminal for VIA Rail.
1 January 1929	On amalgamation with two adjacent municipalities, Vancouver becomes Canada's third-largest city, with nearly one-quarter of a million people.
22 July 1931	Vancouver Airport and Seaplane Harbour officially open.

4 December 1936	Vancouver's City Hall opens.
25 May 1939	The third, and present, Hotel Vancouver opens on its present site, just a few days before King George VI and Queen Elizabeth stay there. The city names its newest park Queen Elizabeth Park.
6 August 1940	Theatre Under The Stars begins in Stanley Park, a much-loved tradition.
9 October 1944	The *St Roch*, a vessel operated by the Royal Canadian Mounted Police, arrives back in Vancouver from Halifax, having gone through the Northwest Passage in both directions. Shortly afterwards, the St Roch sails through the Panama Canal, becoming the first ship to circumnavigate North America.
15 July 1959	Queen Elizabeth and Prince Philip officiate at the opening of the Deas Island Tunnel, now called the Massey Tunnel.
10 September 1965	Simon Fraser University opens.
1986	EXPO '86, marking Vancouver's centennial, attracts 21 million visitors in six months and puts Vancouver in the spotlight around the world.
1996	New terminal opens at Vancouver International Airport.
21 April 2001	Bjossa, the two-year-old female orca, moves from the Vancouver Aquarium to Sea World in San Diego, California. Bjossa was the last live killer whale left at the Aquarium, where she became a member in 1980.
2003	Vancouver selected as the host city for the 2010 Winter Olympic Games.
23 January 2006	After eight years of Liberal government, the Conservative Party wins the general election.
2007	Vancouver celebrates its 150th birthday.

Politics

Canada is a confederation with a parliamentary democracy. In the general election of January 2006, the Conservatives led by Stephen Harper gained enough votes to form a minority government, ending eight years of rule by the middle-of-the-road Liberal Party, headed by Jean Chretien.

BC's turbulent politics are a source of constant astonishment and amusement to the rest of the country (there are ten major provinces in Canada, of which BC is one, each of which has its own Premier, and three territories, one of which is administered by Inuit people).

From 1991 to 2001, the New Democrats held power. In 2000, Ujjal Dosanjh, an Indo-Canadian, replaced Glen Clark as the leader of the NDP and became Premier of BC. In May 2001, the Liberal Party won the provincial election and its leader, Gordon Campbell, a former Vancouver mayor, became Premier of the province – he was also re-elected in 2005. The ratio of women and university graduates in local politics is the highest in BC history. Time will reveal the results these liberalising troops will have on the province's fortunes.

The province's lively political scene is reflected in microcosm in Vancouver, its largest city. For years, left-leaning members of the city council have been engaged in an ideological battle with the right, with middle-of-the-road councillors running the gauntlet. In the 2005 city elections, Sam Sullivan, a quadriplegic and active city councillor for years, replaced former mayor Philip Owen.

BC's 19th-century Parliament building

Culture and events

Vancouver plays host to a full programme of festivals, exhibitions, sporting events and other special celebrations. Most of them are concentrated in the summer, but there is hardly a month of the year when there isn't something special going on. For more information, contact Tourism Vancouver (tel: (604) 683 2000; www.tourismvancouver.com).

In a vibrant city like Vancouver, some people work on Friday, ski on Saturday and sail on Sunday. Possibilities abound for the best in opera, art, theatre, music and cinema on a Saturday evening.

FESTIVALS AND SPECIAL EVENTS
January
Polar Bear Swim
Every New Year's Day more than 2,000 Vancouverites and visitors plunge into the chilly winter waters of English Bay.

Chinese New Year
A colourful celebration of old and modern traditions by Vancouver's Oriental community, highlighted by the Dragon Parade in Chinatown (end January/beginning February).

February/March
Vancouver Playhouse International Wine Festival (Various venues)
Features 500 international wines (late February/early March).

May
The Cloverdale Rodeo
One of the largest rodeos on the continent, held at the fairgrounds over Victoria Day (24 May or preceding weekend).

Vancouver International Children's Festival
Vanier Park
A sea of candy-striped tents transforms the park into a wonderland of theatre, music, dance, puppetry, mime and acrobatics. Runners from all over the world compete in the **Vancouver International Marathon**.

June
Alcan Dragon Boat Festival
A weekend of racing and entertainment.

Vancouver International Jazz Festival
Big names in jazz perform at 40 venues in and around the city.

Gastown has a two-day New Orleans-style street festival.

Bard on the Beach Shakespeare Festival
Different beach venues (June–September).

July
Canada Day
Entertainment and a spectacular fireworks show centred in Canada Place (1st).

Dancing on the Edge Festival
A ten-day dance festival, centred on the Firehall Arts Centre.

Vancouver Folk Music Festival
Three days of performances by local and international singers, musicians and storytellers.
Various venues.

Vancouver International Comedy Festival
Featuring a diverse collection of comic performers from around the world.

HSBC Celebration of Light
A spectacular international fireworks competition over English Bay.

August
Abbotsford Air Show
Abbotsford Airport
Aerial acrobatics, skydiving and wing-walkers fill the skies.

Pacific National Exhibition Concerts
Agricultural exhibitions and an amusement park take over the PNE Grounds for two weeks.

Air Canada Championship
Northview
This PGA tournament draws golfers from many countries.

September
The Fringe
Vancouver's theatre festival features 100 groups from around the world.

Vancouver International Film Festival
One of the country's best.

October
Mid-Autumn Moon Festival
A Chinese cultural celebration, including a lantern festival. Traditional **Thanksgiving** celebrations take place at the Burnaby Village Museum (*tel: (604) 293 6501; www.burnabyparksrec.org*).

December
Festival of Lights
The central areas of VanDusen Gardens ablaze with lights.

Christmas Carol Ship Parade
Greater Vancouver boat owners sail around the harbour in decorated craft.

Christmas at Canada Place
In support of local children's charities.

Impressions

*'You think BC means Before Christ. But it doesn't.
I'm sitting, wildly surmising, on the edge of the Pacific,
gazing at mountains which are changing colour every
two minutes in the most surprising way.
Nature here is half-Japanese.'*

RUPERT BROOKE

English poet, 1913

What to bring

Vancouver has become such a meeting ground of east and west and of business and sports, that almost any wardrobe is acceptable on any occasion. Some women wear fox fur jackets and sandals to the office, while others wear parkas and running shoes. Shorts for both

Coal Harbour, Vancouver

THE ALIENATING

Mist rolls slowly back up the field
a retreating ghost army under
the mother-of-pearl-ringed moon
down the wide aisle of massed
trees ragged palisades of sheer darkness
jet against the prickling sky where
stars keep remote counsel beyond
the perimeters of the wind.

Unbending pioneers
wrestled this farm from the forest
broke the deathgrip of stumps
worried the sour dirt arable
danced often in that silvered-roofed barn
to the fiddle's plangent whine
whirled through squares and circles
when toil stung them hungry for frolic.

But this is a crueller night and time
we spin to more-cynical music
it hammers its city-spawned rhythms
against the ribs of the farmhouse
   behind me
I crouch in limbo beyond the
   window lights
a sudden stranger to both worlds
straining for the thoughts of Sascha
   the dog
and Friendly the sheep, chewing his
   slow dreams.

PETER TROWER

An unusual way of getting around

here. Clothes are generally more expensive than in the USA, but cheaper than in Europe.

Driving and parking

More than 80 per cent of the travellers in BC are motorists. Driving is on the right, with passing on the left. The use of seat belts is mandatory. Right turns are permitted on red lights, after the vehicle has come to a full stop. City streets, freeways and country roads are well maintained.

Vancouver is becoming more crowded. Rush hour seems to be getting longer and parking downtown more challenging. Many parking meters are restricted during rush hours. There are plenty of big car parks indoors and out, but on busy days it may take a while to find a space. To Europeans, Vancouver drivers may seem almost

sexes are fine as leisurewear in summer, but a sweater is often welcome after the sun sets over the Pacific. An umbrella, raincoat and water-resistant footwear can be useful any time of the year, but more so in winter. Layered clothes are practical for trekking up the North Shore mountains or for boating. Don't worry if you haven't brought what you need, for practically everything is sold

Totem poles in Stanley Park

Canadian couples are used to sleeping in double beds, but many rooms have two beds for the asking. Vancouverites usually eat salads before the main course, and green, Caesar and Greek salads are very popular. BC now produces some excellent wines, so Vancouverites are beginning to steer away from imported wines in favour of BC labels.

Smoking on the street, once considered bad form, is now common, as most office buildings do not permit smoking, even in lounge areas. Please smoke in designated areas only.

Some of the dour Scots who once settled this area have left a legacy of appearing unapproachable – or maybe it is a remnant of the Wild West, where any stranger was subject to suspicion. Unlike their Seattle cousins, archaically sedate, Victorians even more so, although driving manners appear to be deteriorating.

Local customs

Vancouver is an orderly city. People usually queue patiently at bus stops and taxi stands. Pedestrians use zebra crossings, as they have the right of way at intersections. Drivers rarely honk their horns, a ticketable offence, even when the traffic is reminiscent of downtown Bangkok at rush hour. If you ask for directions, remember that streets are usually referred to by just the main part of the name – 'Seymour Street' will therefore be known as 'Seymour'.

A RUN THROUGH STANLEY PARK

The cedar hand, wind nodded,
Caressed my arm and sought,
It seemed, my company.

For greeting or chastisement
At my ungreen intrusion?
Habit fit that path to pounding pace;

Yet these verdant curtains
May flail my fondness with fret
That I break the filtered, falling shaft

And sever
The thrust
Too rare in this soft scene.

BRUCE I BURNETT

Vancouverites seem reluctant to be the first to say hello, although they usually respond well to friendly people, and though they pretend to be puritan at times, the doorman at almost every downtown hotel will accept a $5 tip and keep your car nearby for you at no additional charge.

On the quiet, most residents of Vancouver admit their city is one of the most beautiful in the world. Few venture into the great outdoors during the dark, rainy days of winter, though some jog compulsively right through thunderstorms without losing pace. In the rain, it is a little easier to distinguish the locals; they're usually the ones without umbrellas.

Many visitors find the great patches of wilderness in Greater Vancouver, particularly on the North Shore, more than adequate for a short visit. But travellers seeking solitude may want to head into the hinterland, where the people are friendlier and nature's creations are unspoilt.

Impressions

The Wild Pacific Trail

Areas of Vancouver

Greater Vancouver is bounded by the North Shore mountains to the north, the Strait of Georgia to the west and the American border to the south. As more people move to the city, the fertile farmlands of the Fraser Valley to the east are fast being replaced by suburban development.

Downtown Vancouver

In addition to the main business and shopping area, the city centre has several different sections. Gastown, the renovated original part of the city, contains souvenir shops, restaurants and art galleries. **Robson Street** has several blocks of upmarket shops and restaurants with more of the same including high-end art galleries along South Granville Street. Chinatown has a colourful collection of shops and restaurants especially lively at weekends. Yaletown is an area of old warehouses, recently renovated to house restaurants, galleries and studios of artists, architects and designers.

As a result of large-scale immigration, various ethnic enclaves have developed in Vancouver, and shops and restaurants have opened to cater to their tastes. There are also a lot of East Indians along the southern end of Main Street, Greeks along West Broadway, Germans on Fraser Street and Italians on Commercial Drive, and around Hastings and Nanaimo streets. There is a tiny Japantown on Powell Street and an equally small French-language pocket on West 16th Avenue.

The city's economic watershed is often held to be Cambie Street. To oversimplify, west of that north–south route live doctors, architects, business executives and college professors; east are sawmill workers, waitresses and factory workers.

Kerrisdale

Gentrification in recent years has polished the image of this neighbourhood, which is now smarter and shinier than Kitsilano to the north.

Kitsilano

Kitsilano, especially along West Fourth Avenue, was once a hotbed of the hippy era, with its pot smokers, tie-dyers, vegetarians, protesters and peaceniks. It still remains the most laid-back neighbourhood in town.

Shaughnessy

In this wealthy neighbourhood, streets lined with towering trees curve around imposing mansions. Shaughnessy was established by the Canadian Pacific Railway a century ago as a residential enclave for executives. In the poorest section, in downtown eastside with Hastings and Carrall streets as its hub, a committed group of residents is fighting to improve conditions.

Suburbia

Nearly two dozen suburbs surround Vancouver. **Richmond**, the site of Vancouver International Airport, is a rapidly growing city to the south. Surrey, a huge municipality on the south side of the Fraser River, is also expanding fast, partly due to the recent extension of the SkyTrain rapid transit. The southern part of **Surrey** is very attractive, with dairy farms dotted around the green, rolling hills.

A quiet, high-income, no-industry, residential area, West Vancouver has some of the most agreeable suburbs.

Downtown Vancouver

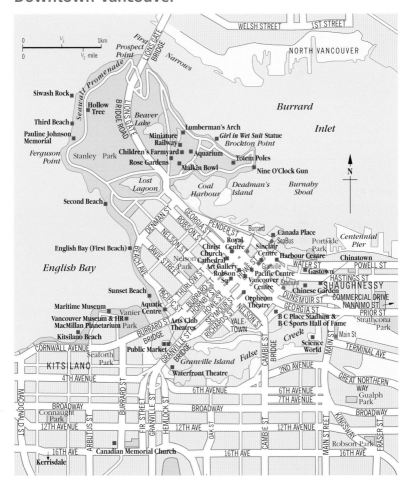

Areas of BC

The Rockies

This region stretches northwest from the 49th parallel along the Alberta border. The main highway follows the Columbia River through the broad valley of the Rocky Mountain Trench.

Cariboo Chilcotin

This region stretches from the fiords of the Pacific to the forested foothills of the Cariboo mountains.

High Country

This vast region offers lakes and rivers, glaciated mountain passes, waterfalls, forests and arid desert plateaux.

Kootenay Country

This region nestles between the fertile farmlands of the Okanagan Similkameen and the Rockies.

North by Northwest

This vast area encompasses one-third of BC and stretches from the Rockies to Haida Gwaii (the Queen Charlotte Islands).

Okanagan Similkameen

This small, L-shaped region is situated along the American border midway between the Rockies and the Pacific. The Okanagan Valley produces much of the province's wines.

Peace River–Alaska Highway

This region is set between the foothills of the Rockies and the Alberta prairie. The Alaska Highway runs from Dawson Creek (Mile Zero) northwest through Fort Nelson and Liard Valley to Alaska.

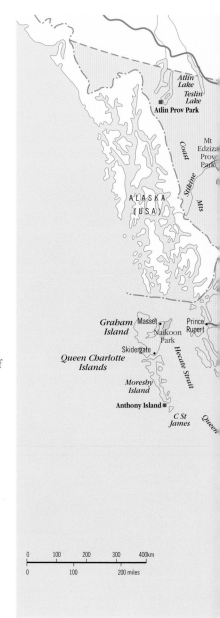

British Columbia

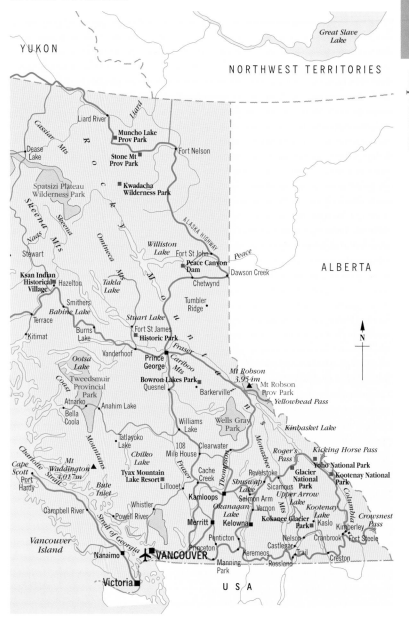

Vancouver

Vancouver, commonly called the Gateway to the Pacific, is almost entirely surrounded by water. To the north is Burrard Inlet, an ice-free harbour where freighters fly flags from many nations. To the south, the Fraser River flows west into the Strait of Georgia, which separates Vancouver and the rest of the mainland from Vancouver Island. As a prairie farmer remarked, 'Vancouver would be great, if the view wasn't blocked by the mountains'. The sheltering ranges attract grey clouds that shower the city with 140cm (55in) of rain a year, resulting in fresh air and lush green landscapes. The clouds frost the peaks with snow for city skiing five months a year.

Metropolitan Vancouver covers 3,000sq km (1,158sq miles), including the suburbs of North Vancouver, West Vancouver, Burnaby, Coquitlam, Port Coquitlam, Port Moody, Pitt Meadows, Richmond, White Rock, Delta, New Westminster, Surrey and Langley.

Although Vancouver is Canada's third-largest city (after Toronto and

Mounties are everywhere!

Montreal), the many waterways, mountains and parks lend the illusion of space.

While the past has been largely the story of seeking and selling natural resources, new industries are emerging. Local skills now produce sightseeing submarines, satellite-sensing equipment, computer software and data terminal designs.

A growing tourism industry draws some visitors back as residents. Hotels continue to spring up in a city centre of skyscrapers. Well-developed facilities and roadways allow visitors and residents to ski in the morning, sail in the afternoon and enjoy opera in the evening. Even business seems a sport in this city, which has one of the most speculative stock markets in the world.

Most people come to Vancouver for the scenery, so first select one of its many vantage points for an overview of the city. People who like to keep their feet firmly planted on the ground may prefer to stroll along the promenade deck at Canada Place, a good orientation spot. With its five white sails jutting out into the harbour, this city landmark features a dozen markers indicating sites of interest around the city. You can also enjoy spectacular views from some downtown city buildings. Another great way to orient yourself is to take an aerial tour and get a real bird's-eye view.

The view from the top of the Harbour Centre

Aerial sightseeing
Harbour Air
BC's largest seaplane company packages eight tours, varying from a half-hour flight over the city centre to a six-hour round trip to Vancouver Island.
Tel: (604) 274 1277, freephone (800) 665 0212; www.harbour-air.com

Helijet
Scenic city and wilderness tours, departing from downtown and Grouse Mountain. Options range from the 20-minute West Coast Spectacular to the Grand Glacier Tour. Glacier tours are seasonal, May to September, and weather dependent.
*455 Waterfront Rd, Richmond.
Tel: (604) 270 1484, freephone (800) 665 4354; www.helijet.com*

Sundance Balloons
Early morning and sunset flights over BC landscapes with champagne. Flights run from May to October and off season (as weather permits).

*Tel: (604) 533 7552;
www.sundanceballoons.com*

Bird's-eye viewpoints
Cloud Nine
The price of a meal or a drink at the Cloud Nine restaurant, atop the 42-storey Empire Landmark Hotel, includes a 360-degree view of Vancouver.
1400 Robson St. Tel: (604) 687 0511.

Harbour Centre
Get your bearings from above at The Lookout!, a revolving viewing deck at the top of the Harbour Centre.
*555 West Hastings St. Tel: (604) 689 0421; www.vancouverlookout.com.
Open: summer 8.30am–10.30pm, winter 9am–9pm. Admission charge.*

Vistas on the Bay
Gourmets of both food and scenery love the revolving Vistas restaurant at the top of the Renaissance Hotel.
1133 West Hastings St. Tel: (604) 689 9211. Viewing free, opens at 5.30pm.

The charm of BC's beaches

Vancouver's beaches are an essential part of the city's outdoor culture. They provide the perfect venue for cycling, rollerblading, beach volleyball, or, on a more relaxing note, a romantic stroll, and, of course, sunbathing.

On New Year's Day in Vancouver, however, around 2,000 locals dash into English Bay for the Polar Bear Swim. No one lingers long; they dress quickly and head indoors to recuperate from the chilling waters.

But summer is another story. Beaches become crowded with swimmers, sand-castle builders, frisbee players, kite flyers and sunseekers who want to have fun. An occasional canine slips

The beaches around the city provide idyllic recreational spaces for urbanites

Kitsilano Beach

in without permission, and squirrels sometimes appear hoping for handouts. Towards sunset, an entrepreneur with a metal detector in hand may sift the sands hoping for hidden treasures.

Although many people bring picnics, alcohol is not allowed; but it is rumoured that every now and then a thermos brings in wine masquerading as Kool-Aid. There are sandy, gravel and pebble shores. English Bay's Sunset Beach is ribboned with gigantic trunks from rainforest trees that escaped log booms, a reminder that timber is a key industry here. The logs are great for leaning on, and they provide some privacy. Some are big enough for a single sunbather to stretch right out on top.

Although the sun is tempered by refreshing offshore breezes, it is wise to wear a strong sunscreen for protection against the direct rays and those reflected off the sea and sand. West Vancouver's Ambleside Beach is one of the few city beaches to permit barbecues. It is wonderful to roast hot dogs and marshmallows around a flickering fire as the Lions Gate Bridge lights up and the sunset fades into the darkening evening sky over English Bay.

Beaches

Although beachcombing is a pleasant pastime come rain or shine in winter, Vancouver beaches are at their best in summer. From Victoria Day to Labour Day, lifeguards supervise the city's ten swimming beaches from 11.30am to 9pm. There is no admission charge to the beaches, and changing rooms, toilets and refreshment stands are found in many convenient locations.

English Bay (First Beach)

Fifteen minutes from downtown, English Bay sports some fine beaches.
At the foot of Davie & Denman Sts.

Kitsilano Beach

Kitsilano Beach has a heated outdoor saltwater pool overlooking English Bay. Nearby Jericho Beach, Locarno Beach and Spanish Banks are favourites with windsurfers. There is adequate parking, and picnic tables are scattered along the beach.
Southwest of the Burrard St Bridge.

Second Beach

This beach features a pool that protects children from the currents. There are areas for barbecues and for playing soccer, football, volleyball and baseball.
In Stanley Park, north of Sunset Beach.

Sunset Beach

At this beach, the closest to downtown, summer sunsets are glorious. Residents and visitors congregate on giant logs on the beach or sip sundowners at the front tables in the nearby English Bay Café and the Sylvia Hotel.
At the corner of Pacific Ave & Jervis St.

Third Beach

This isolated beach is relatively quiet, a haven for those looking to get away.
On the west side of Stanley Park, north of Second Beach & Ferguson Point.

Wreck Beach

This beach has unrivalled natural beauty. A steep trail (not easy to find, ask for directions) winds down to the water from North West Marine Drive to this unspoilt wild strand, the only nudist beach in the Lower Mainland.
On the tip of the Point Grey peninsula near the University of British Columbia.

For information, contact Kits Tower in season (tel: (604) 738 8535); and Vancouver Aquatic Centre off season (tel: (604) 665 3424); www. city.vancouver.bc.ca/parks/rec/beaches

Chinatown

Vancouver's thriving Chinatown, a ten-minute walk from the city centre, stretches over six blocks, north to south down Main Street to the Georgia Street viaduct, and east to west from Gore Street to Carrall Street. Millions of dollars change hands here, in hundreds of businesses ranging from banks to food to electronics. Chinese immigrants bring in an estimated $2 billion to BC every year.

Chinatown is home to a few thousand permanent residents, mostly elderly. Most Chinese Canadians live elsewhere, but come to Chinatown to bank, shop and eat. The streets bustle with activity. Shops overflowing with rosewood furniture, bamboo and wickerware, jade jewellery and porcelain stand cheek-by-jowl with herbal pharmacies and authentic Chinese restaurants, most of which serve excellent food at reasonable prices.
*For more information:
www.vancouver-chinatown.com*

Colourful signs, Chinatown

Chinese Cultural Centre

Situated between Carrall and Columbia streets (*see p30*), the Chinese Cultural Centre houses changing exhibitions of traditional culture and local history and sponsors the annual Chinese New Year Parade.
50 East Pender St. Tel: (604) 658 8850; www.cccvan.com. Open: Tue–Sun 11am–5pm. Closed Mon. Free admission.

Dr Sun Yat-Sen Park and Garden

This garden (*see pp30–31*), opened for Expo '86, was created in classical Chinese style and is a harmonious blend of plants and space, with numerous terraces, pavilions and walkways.
578 Carrall St. Tel: (604) 662 3207. Hours vary according to season. Call for current opening times. Admission charge.

Sam Kee Building

*See p30.
At the southwest corner of Pender & Carrall sts. Not open to the public, but can be viewed from outside.*

Walk: Chinatown

Vancouver's Chinatown (see also p29), the second largest in North America (at present) after San Francisco, crams a lot of life into six city blocks, a ten-minute walk from the city centre.

Allow 2 hours for walking and another hour for dim sum *(see pp166–7).*

Begin this tour at the southwest corner of Carrall and Pender sts.

1 Sam Kee Building

Built in 1913, the Sam Kee Building may be the narrowest building in the world (1.8m by 30m/6ft by 98ft), and is listed in *Guinness World Records*. The two-storey building, once living quarters for a Chinese family, is now home to Jack Chow Insurance and a group of architects upstairs who own the building.

2 Chinese Cultural Centre

In the next block east, the Chinese Cultural Centre, marked by an enormous red gateway, houses a library and rooms for language lessons, *tai chi*,

Chinese painting, lantern making and frequently changing exhibits of Oriental and Canadian art.
Behind the CCC lies the Dr Sun Yat-Sen Park and Garden.

3 Dr Sun Yat-Sen Park and Garden

High, whitewashed walls hide this pocket of peace from the bustling city beyond. Modelled after the classic scholars' gardens of the Ming Dynasty (1368–1644), the Taoist balance of yin and yang (light and shadow, smooth and rough, large and small) creates perfect harmony. This quiet,

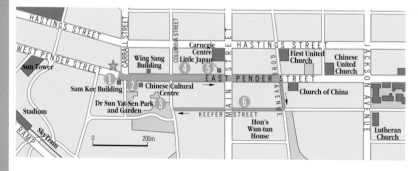

secluded sanctuary shelters varied vistas of pebbled patios, moon gates, lattice windows, see-through shrubbery, placid milky-jade pools and craggy grey limestone.
Cross Pender St.

4 Pender Street

Across Pender Street, the Wing Sang Building, housing the Yen Lock Restaurant, is the oldest structure in Chinatown, dating from 1889.

Both sides of Pender are lined with Mandarin, Cantonese and Szechuan restaurants, and shops selling such imported goods as wickerware, parasols, porcelain, bamboo birdcages and jade jewellery. Prices are reasonable, and browsers are welcome. At the Chinese pharmacies, you can see experts mixing potions of herbs, ginseng root, dried cuttlefish, powdered antler velvet and other exotic ingredients for infusions to alleviate everything from influenza to impotence. Many Westerners now take ginseng and royal jelly.
Continue east along Pender St.

5 Little Japan

At 173 East Pender, down a few stairs, is Yeu Hua Crafts Ltd, specialists in arts and crafts from China. Their business card says 'wholesale welcome', so prices are probably negotiable, even though they sound reasonable. The store stocks a great selection of attractive rosewood furniture in various sizes, delicate porcelain and cloisonné, silk

The Dr Sun Yat-Sen Garden, a taste of the Orient in Vancouver's Chinatown

embroidery and paper goods. And Yeu Hua will ship everything home for you.
Cross Main St, still on Pender St, turn right on Gore Ave, walk a block to Keefer St and turn right again.

6 Keefer Street

Here, the predominant aroma announces windows of Chinese pastries. Most pastry shops have a room at the back for a tasty cup of tea and a snack (the coffee is usually mediocre). On the south side of Keefer stands a shopping centre, with Hon's Wun-tun House (great soup and noodles for low prices; cash only, no alcohol) at street level. As it happens, the big supermarket in the basement is not nearly as much fun as street shopping.
Follow Keefer St two blocks west back to the Dr Sun Yat-Sen Park and Garden.

NEARBY

Church of China, Sun Tower.

Chinese Canadians

During the 5th century, several Chinese Buddhist priests visited a country they called Fu Sang, now believed to have been the west coast of Canada. But the first real wave of Chinese immigrants did not arrive until the 1858 gold rush. Some stayed and started farms and laundries, or worked in the salmon canneries, sawmills and coal mines. Some 25 years later, 10,000 Chinese workers were imported to lay tracks for the cross-Canada railway. Racism forced Chinese families to live crowded together in a small area, the beginning of today's Chinatown in Vancouver. Now more than 332,560 Chinese Canadians live in Metropolitan Vancouver and others have settled elsewhere in the province.

Although 50 per cent of newcomers to BC are from other Canadian provinces, about 22,000 Asian immigrants are estimated to arrive each year. Most of the

Tranquillity in the middle of Vancouver's thriving Chinatown

Exotic ingredients await you in Chinatown

people arriving from Hong Kong and Taiwan bring considerable wealth, skills, willingness to work and sophistication.

Some Chinese come here because they like the space, the cleanliness, the order and the economic opportunities. Many Hong Kong families, concerned about Hong Kong's return to China in 1997, sent their teenage offspring to study in Canadian schools and universities, to provide them with more career opportunities. Others are investing capital in property, manufacturing, electronics and other ventures in BC so that they might take up residence here in the future.

Fortunately, the descendants of the original British settlers in BC are developing greater tolerance of other races. About 25 per cent of children entering school here speak Cantonese or Mandarin as their mother tongue, and young Vancouverites are no longer concerned whether their friends come from an Asian or European background. The highest office in the province, that of lieutenant-governor, was held, until recently, by David Lam, a highly respected and admired Chinese immigrant.

For more information contact the Chinese Cultural Centre, *tel: (604) 658 8880; www.cccvan.com*

Walk: Gastown

Gastown, a five-minute hike from the city centre, is the oldest part of Vancouver. The area was designated a heritage site in 1971. Old gas-style lamps and young maple trees line cobblestoned Water Street, whose three blocks comprise the heart of Gastown. For more information visit www.gastown.org

Allow at least 2 hours.

Begin this tour at the corner of Richards and Water sts. Head east on the north side of Water St.

1 The Landing

The first stop, The Landing, is an award-winning heritage structure containing a dozen elegant shops clustered around a central lobby, whose arched floor-to-ceiling window frames the North Shore mountains. A shiny escalator leads from one polished oak floor to the other. Head to the lower level, pick up a local newspaper or the *New York Times* at the Fleet Street news-stand, and savour a cappuccino and muffin, a good melange of America and Europe, at the adjacent friendly café or the 1950s-style diner at the east end of the building.

Landmark shops sell Scottish tartans, Belgian chocolates, Japanese lingerie, cut and potted flowers, Canadian winter clothes, gold jewellery handcrafted on site, designer clothes, toys for children, embroidered Victoria cushions, maple-wood salad bowls and smoked salmon packed for shipping. *Continue along Water St.*

2 Inuit Gallery

Water Street is lined with dozens of shops selling everything from souvenir sweatshirts to Art Deco furniture. The most exciting stop is the Inuit Gallery, a few doors east of The Landing, which houses an impressive array of Inuit sculpture and Northwest native art. The so-called naive art recalls the way Inuit families used to live in harmony with their harsh land, expressed in soapstone and whalebone sculptures. The shop also sells Northwest native Canadian cedar carvings, buttoned blankets and ceremonial masks.

A little further along on the left is the steam clock.

3 Steam Clock

Dedicated to the citizens of Vancouver in 1977, the 2-ton steam clock was built by Gillett & Johnston of Croydon, England. The movement was based on an 1875 vintage design, and has a 19kg (42lb) gold-plated pendulum.

A machine in a nearby basement is triggered by clockwork every 15 minutes, and little pins play a Westminster Chimes tune which electronically blows five steam whistles. The steam manifold for the whistles sits on top of the cube housing the four dials, each highlighted by four enamelled copper dogwood flowers. A 24-carat gold-plated frame surrounds the dials which glow at night.
Continue along Water St.

4 The Courtyard

In the next block meander through The Courtyard, where Vancouver architects, tour operators and lawyers work behind huge glass windows. The outdoor café and delicatessen up the stairs provides a pleasant pause with a view across the harbour.
At the end of Water St, turn right into Carrall St.

5 Maple Tree Square

In Maple Tree Square stands the statue of 'Gassy' Jack Deighton, a garrulous Yorkshireman who built a saloon for lumber mill workers on the site of the Broghes building behind in 1867. The building is made with bricks from China that were used as ballast on sailing ships calling for timber at the Hastings Mill. Deighton, who had arrived in Vancouver with his wife, six dollars, a few sticks of furniture and a yellow dog, was an overnight success. Because he was so talkative and optimistic about prospects for Burrard Inlet, locals called him 'Gassy Jack', and the ramshackle collection of huts and shops surrounding the saloon was dubbed Gastown. Jack's statue faces the old Europe Hotel, a good example of the renovated Victorian buildings in Gastown.
Turn west through the Gaoler's Mews.

6 Gaoler's Mews

This cobblestoned courtyard is where Vancouver's first gaol once stood. A little further along, Blood Alley marks the site of many dastardly deeds during the settlement of the Wild West.

The south side of Water Street is also lined with shops and restaurants. Water Street restaurants cover the cuisines of Italy, France, Kenya, India and America. Just off Water Street at 217 Carrall, you'll find The Irish Heather, a gastropub serving updated Irish food.
Return along Water St to The Landing.

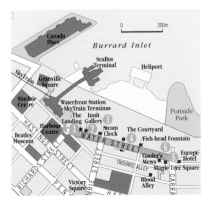

NEARBY

Portside Park, Beatles Museum.

Trolley tour: Gastown to Chinatown

The Trolley Tour is the best preview of Vancouver's varied attractions. The bright red-and-gold non-polluting gas-operated trolleys, decorated in oak and brass, are replicas of those used in the 1890s. There are 24 stops, many of them at major hotels. The first stop is in Gastown, but you can start your tour anywhere on the trolley line. Trolley Tours partners with the Gray Line of Vancouver's Double Decker line – your ticket is accepted on both the trolley and the double decker buses.

Allow about 2 hours for the tour if you don't take advantage of the stops.

1 Gastown
The heart of old Vancouver and home to the Steam Clock (*see pp34–5*).

2 SeaBus Terminal/The Lookout
Hop on one of Vancouver's passenger ferries or head up to The Lookout! to see Vancouver from above.

3 Canada Place
Home to the IMAX theatre.
The tour makes a loop through downtown, stopping at many of the major hotels, the Art Gallery, and the shopping district.

4 Marriott Pinnacle/Renaissance

5 Hyatt Regency/Melville Street
Two blocks from Robson Street's lively shopping district.

6 Art Gallery (Howe Street), Pacific Centre
The Art Gallery houses a large collection of work by local legend Emily Carr.

7 Holiday Inn (on Helmcken)

8 Quality Inn (on Drake)

9 Marriott/Landis Hotels

10 Sheraton Wall Centre

11 Robson Street (Blue Horizon Hotel)
Tourists and locals alike promenade Robson to take advantage of the varied shopping opportunities.

12 Westin Bayshore
After the Westin the trolley enters Stanley

Park. The route goes around the outside of the park and stops at all the major attractions.

13 Stanley Park

The Rose Gardens are at their showiest between June and October and in late March and April. Visit the Vancouver Aquarium to see the Beluga whales and Spinnaker the dolphin.

14 Stanley Park Totem Poles

A stunning introduction to the history and culture of British Columbia's native people.

15 Stanley Park – Prospect Point

Admire the view from Prospect Point or stop for a bite to eat at one of Stanley Park's fine restaurants.
The trolley leaves Stanley Park at English Bay.

16 English Bay (Beach & Davie)

Popular for sunbathing, beautiful sunset views, and reasonably priced dining.

17 Aquatic Centre/Sunset Beach

Visit this prisitine and quiet beach or take a swim in Vancouver's Olympic-sized pool.
The trolley heads southwest across the Burrard Street Bridge.

18 Vanier Park Stop

For Vancouver Museum, Maritime Museum and Space Centre.

19 Granville Island (Entrance)

Arts, industry and dining are side by side in this colourful market district.
After crossing Granville Island, the trolley goes over the Granville Bridge back towards downtown.

20 Yaletown (Homer & Helmcken)

Vancouver's trendy designer district. High end shopping and dining.

21 Library Square (Homer Street)

This distinctive complex houses government offices, the main library, shopping and cafés.

22 Sandman Inn (Georgia Street)

23 Science World

Catch a big-screen movie at the OMNIMAX Theatre or learn about the world around you. Child friendly.

24 Chinatown

Go from the tranquillity of Dr Sun Yat-Sen Garden to the bustling activity of Chinatown. Or stay onboard and head back to Gastown.

Tours run 8.30am–6pm. Trolleys alternate with double decker buses every 15 minutes. The last tour leaves Gastown at 4.15pm and returns at 6.15pm. Vancouver Trolley offers other themed tours – contact them for tickets and information (tel: (604) 801 5515 or freephone (888) 451 5581; www.vancouvertrolley.com).

The BC art scene

Nature has been and continues to be the dominating influence motivating local artists. It is clearly evident in their work, from the powerful and mysterious moods of old-growth rainforests and totem poles painted by Emily Carr to the subtle watercolour seascapes of Toni Onley.

Emily Carr, born in Victoria in 1871, is acknowledged as the grand matriarch of BC art. Her inspiration came from both the natural surroundings and the original inhabitants, as she travelled the BC coast collecting and portraying a wealth of impressions from First

The Raven and the First Men by Bill Reid

Vancouver Art Gallery on Hornby Street

Nations peoples, their arts and their legends.

Other BC greats include Bill Reid, Reg Davidson and Roy Vickers, who all have a native heritage; European immigrants John Coerner from the former Czechoslovakia, and Bratsa Bonisacho from the former Yugoslavia; Attila Rick Lukacs, originally from Alberta; as well as other talents such as Ross Penhall and Lorraine Yabuki.

Since the 1980s, local artists have expressed a strong commentary on preserving the environment and on controversies focused around fishing, logging and endangered species.

The work of local photographers Jeff Wall, Rodney Graham, Fred Douglas and Marion Penner-Bancroft has earned international renown. And sculptors Roland Brennen and Mowry Baden, using plastics, electronics and other present-day products, have set a new direction for West Coast sculpture with their kinetic creations. In addition to showing the contemporary works of resident painters, sculptors and photographers, local galleries hold regular exhibitions. These include First Nations' cedar carvings and paintings, with their traditional colourful oval designs, Inuit soapstone sculptures from the Arctic, as well as works by the Canadian Group of Seven (*www.groupofsevenart.com*) where Emily Carr was Associate Contemporary Artist, and old European and Asian masters.

Galleries

Vancouver is a young city, and youthful energy and enthusiasm are reflected in the freshness of its art scene, both in traditional West Coast art and in more avant-garde work. Since galleries often close to mount new shows and because some are staffed by volunteers, it is often wise to phone ahead to check opening times.

Downtown

Buschlen-Mowatt Gallery

Dedicated to showcasing museum-quality contemporary artists of regional, national and international significance, with a focus on sculpture.
1445 West Georgia St. Tel: (604) 682 1234; www.buschlenmowatt.ca

Dôrian Rae Collection

Asian and African art and artefacts.
410 Howe St. Tel: (604) 874 6100.

Rendez-vous Gallery

Located opposite the Four Seasons Hotel, the gallery sells paintings, prints and sculptures by emerging and established Canadian artists.
671 Howe St. Tel: (604) 687 7466; www.rendez-vousartgallery.com

Teck Gallery

Features changing exhibitions.
Simon Fraser University, Harbour Centre, 505 West Hastings St. Tel: (604) 681 5881.

Vancouver Art Gallery

A Neoclassical heritage building and a work of art itself, it houses paintings by the early 20th-century Canadian artists known as the Group of Seven; evocative rainforest works by Emily Carr (1871–1945); works by Dutch, Italian, French, German and English masters; and photography, sculpture, graphics and video works.

You can wander around on your own or join a free 20-minute tour. The reference-only library, gift shop and restaurant make the Vancouver Art Gallery a rainy-day special.
750 Hornby St. Tel: (604) 662 4719 for 24-hour information; www.vanartgallery.bc.ca

Gastown

Marion Scott Gallery

Features Inuit sculptures, prints, drawings and wall hangings.
308 Water St. Tel: (604) 685 1934.

Hill's Native Art

Art from Canada's First Nations artists in a variety of mediums – prints, carvings, totems, beadwork and more. Hill's will ship your purchases for you.

165 Water Street; www.hillsnativeart.com.
Open: daily 9am–9pm.

Inuit Gallery

Exhibits and sells excellent traditional
Inuit masterworks, Cape Dorset Inuit
sculpture and West Coast native
Indian works.
206 Cambie St. Tel: (604) 688 7323.

Granville Island

Charles H Scott Gallery

Located in the Emily Carr Institute of
Art and Design, the gallery mounts
travelling shows. You can walk through
the school and look at students' work.
1399 Johnston St, Granville Island.
Tel: (604) 844 3809.

Lattimer Gallery

Sells many current works by First
Nation artists.
1590 W 2nd Ave. Tel: (604) 732 4556;
www.lattimergallery.com

South Granville

Atelier Gallery

Sells contemporary art.
2421 Granville St. Tel: (604) 732 3021.

Bau-Xi Gallery

Features Canadian contemporary art.
Be sure to look upstairs as well.
3045 Granville St. Tel: (604) 733 7011.

Catriona Jeffries

Exhibits and sells interesting
contemporary local and imported art.
3149 Granville St. Tel: (604) 736 1554.

Douglas Reynolds Gallery

Historic and contemporary First
Nations masks, jewellery, prints and
other fine arts.

2335 Granville Street.
Tel: (604) 731 9292.

Equinox Gallery

Features international contemporary
shows.
2321 Granville St. Tel: (604) 736 2405.

Petley Jones

Features contemporary and older works
in dealer's stock.
2235 Granville St. Tel: (604) 732 5353.

Other galleries

Diane Farris Gallery

Contemporary painting and sculpture
from up-and-comers to established
artists.
274 E 1st Street.
Tel: (604) 736 1054;
www.dianefarrisgallery.com

Federation of Canadian Artists

Juried exhibits of original paintings by
Canadian artists.
1241 Cartwright St.
Tel: (604) 681 8534.

Western Front

The premier multi-discipline gallery
in Canada, with artist-managed
gallery space.
303 E 8th Ave. Tel: (604) 878 7563.

Surrey Art Gallery

An eclectic programme of temporary
exhibitions alongside its permanent
collection.
13750 88th Ave, Surrey.
Tel: (604) 501 5566.

Canoe Pass Gallery

Gifted Canadian native artists.
115–3866 Bayview Pier in Steveston.
Tel: (604) 272 0095.

Walk: Art in public places

Vancouver's neighbourhoods are full of outdoor art and exceptional architecture. A walk along the waterfront at English Bay or the False Creek side of the city reveals diverse works – fountains, sculpture in a variety of media, architecture from art deco to post modern … The City of Vancouver has produced a detailed guide that takes sturdy walkers 13km (8 miles) around the perimeter of downtown. Less ambitious art lovers may want to focus only on a specific district. A plan of the entire walk, with a map, is available at www.city.vancouver.bc.ca/commsvcs/oca/PublicArt/pdf/ShorelineWalk.PDF

The first 12 stops in the walk are along the waterfront at Burrard Inlet. Start in Coal Harbour on the pier Canada Place.

1 Canada Place

With its soaring, sail-like roof, this opened as the Canada Pavilion at Expo '86. Keep an eye out for the information panels that retell the area's history – and don't overlook the stunning views.

2 *Salute to the Lions of Vancouver*

On the West side of Canada Place, find Gathie Falk's leaping lions. The two lions reflect the Lions Gate Bridge and the Lions Mountains, known to local First Nations as the Two Sisters. *Cross the street and walk up the pedestrian area to Hornby Street.*

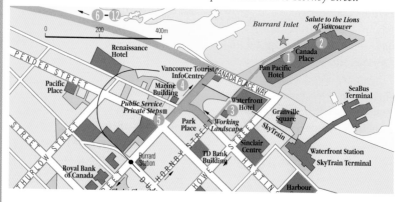

3 *Working Landscape*

Three rotating platforms by Daniel Laskarin complete their full revolutions in one-hour, eight-hour, and 24-hour increments.
Head down Hastings towards Burrard Street.

4 The Marine Building

The Marine Building at 335 Burrard Street is an Art Deco gem, built in 1930. Notice the sea-life inspired surface decorations in the entrance and take note of the elaborate lift doors.

5 *Public Service/Private Steps*

Alan Storey's *Public Service/Private Steps* is just across Hastings from the Marine Building at 401 Burrard. The moving cubes mimic the activity of the people and the elevators inside the building.

6 Harbour Green Shoreline

Stroll down the waterfront and enjoy the Harbour Green Shoreline Walk. This seawall park was designed to be an expanding home for public art – look for Liz Magor's *Light Shed*, John Clement's *Kini's Playground* and Dan Corson's *One in Light* – a fountain that reflects changing colours at night.

7 *Weave*

At the foot of Jervis Street towards the west end of the park, look down to find one component of *Weave* by Douglas Senft. The rings represent the staggering size of old growth trees.

Weave includes other references to British Columbia's natural history.

8 *Make West*

Along Coal Harbour Quay between Nicola Street and Cardero, Bill Pachet's *Make West* recreates the history of Coal Harbour with a series of stones, plaques and bronze castings set in the walkway.

9 Bayshore Waterfront Walkway and Gardens

Just north of the Westin Bayshore Hotel, look for the steel and glass shelters that reroute rainwater back to the inlet. Take a break on one of the benches in this plaza and enjoy the views and the gardens.

10 *Leaf Stream*

A few steps further down the walkway, there's *Leaf Stream*, Douglas Senft's cascading fountain at the foot of Georgia Street. The water flows over recognisable cast-iron icons of Canada – maple leaves.

11 *Search*

Enter Denovan Park at the foot of Denman Street and have a seat next to the subject of *Search* by S Seward Johnson Jr.

12 *Solo*

End this portion of the walk at *Solo*, also in Denovan Park. This abstract piece by Natalie McHaffie expresses motion in shiny stainless steel and cedar planks.

Gardens and parks

Every February, when most of Canada is still covered in ice and snow, the first crocuses of spring poke their heads above ground to take a look at Vancouver and Victoria. The temperate coastal climate, ample sunshine and abundant rainfall encourage and ensure a great diversity of colourful flora. The greenery, which reigns supreme most of the year, is upstaged by riots of colourful blossom in spring and summer.

There are more than 150 gardens and parks in Vancouver, not counting the hundreds of thousands of private yards and gardens. Two of the prettiest public oases in the city differ greatly in character. Wild and rambling Stanley Park (*see pp70–73*) is Western, while the Dr Sun Yat-Sen Chinese Garden (*see pp30–31*) is typically Eastern.

Botanical Gardens at the University of British Columbia

This showcase of plants from around the world includes a physic garden for medicinal herbs, planted around a sundial in the geometric design of a 16th-century herb garden. Horticulturists here have developed such new plants as the Emerald Carpet, a practical, low-spreading ground-cover plant with little flowers. The Arbour Garden provides cool shade where vines abound year round, while the Food Garden grows fruit trees trained in traditional styles, and

the latest vegetables. The Asian Garden features 300 species of rhododendrons, along with kiwi fruit vines and magnolias.
6804 Southwest Marine Drive. Tel: (604) 822 4208; www.ubcbotanicalgarden.org. Open: Mar–Oct 10am–6pm; Nov & Feb 10am–5pm. Closed: Dec–Jan (call for specific dates). Admission charge (free in winter).

Nitobe Memorial Garden

Reflecting the private retreats of Japan, gentle walkways meander through artistically pruned cherry, maple and pine trees, and layouts of sand and rock, to a tiny teahouse. The cherry blossoms in April or May and the iris blooms in late June are spectacular.
Across the street from the UBC Botanical Gardens. Tel: (604) 822 6038; www.nitobe.org. Open: daily 10am–6pm (2.30pm in winter). Admission charge (free in winter).

Park and Tilford Gardens

This privately owned hideaway offers a delightful variety of plantings and landscape themes.

333 Brooksbank Ave, North Vancouver. Tel: (604) 984 8200. Open: daily 9am–sunset. Free admission.

Queen Elizabeth Park

This 52-hectare (128-acre) former stone quarry, transformed into sunken gardens, is a favourite site for bridal couples and wedding photos amid lawns, trees, shrubs and flowers. It is the highest spot in the city (152m/499ft), so views are spectacular. The blossoms are at their best in late May and June, when azaleas and rhododendrons create a brilliant kaleidoscope of colour. An arboretum on the east side showcases trees and shrubs indigenous to the BC coast.

There is also a rose garden, a pitch-and-putt golf course (*tel: (604) 874 8336*), 20 tennis courts, and a restaurant looking out to the city. The Bloedel Floral Conservatory (*tel: (604) 257 8584*), a 20m (66ft) high triodetic dome consisting of 1,490 plexiglas bubbles, houses a tropical garden with more than 100 colourful birds flying free, and an arid area with cacti, and seasonal floral displays.

33rd Ave at Cambie St. Tel: (604) 257 8570; www.city.vancouver.bc.ca/parks/parks/queenelizabeth/. Open: daily 9am–8pm in summer; Oct–mid-Apr 10am–5pm. Admission charge to the conservatory.

VanDusen Botanical Garden

This spectacular 22-hectare (55-acre) garden in the heart of Vancouver has matured into a botanical garden of international stature since opening to the public in 1975. The mild Vancouver climate allows the cultivation of an outstanding plant collection which is a delight at any time of the year. There are over 7,500 different kinds of plants assembled from six continents. Specific garden areas are planted to illustrate botanical relationships, such as the Rhododendron Walk, or geographical origins as in the Sino-Himalayan Garden. These areas are set amid rolling lawns, tranquil lakes and dramatic rock-work, with vistas of the mountains and the Vancouver cityscape.

5251 Oak St, not far from Queen Elizabeth Park. Tel: (604) 878 9274; www.vandusengarden.org. Open: daily 10am–dusk. Admission charge.

VanDusen Botanical Garden

Walk: Pacific Spirit Park

A walk in the wild woods on the edge of the city offers patches of ocean framed by red cedars where squirrels scuffle through the underbrush, birds sing and serenity is all around – just a few of the pleasures of Pacific Spirit Park. Personnel working on the trails are also helpful.

Allow about 2 hours, plus time for birdwatching.

Begin at Chancellor Blvd, where the extra lane for parking begins, just beyond the Pacific Spirit Park sign. Start on the Pioneer Trail, then follow the first right to the Spanish Trail, which meanders through the woods to Spanish Banks Beach or loops back on to the Pioneer Trail to the entrance.

The **Pioneer Trail** and **Spanish Trail** loop, which is about 2km (1¹/₄ miles) long, can be muddy in sections, but this is to be expected in a rainforest. The Spanish Trail heads north into tall trees and undergrowth, and for a while parallels the south edge of a tree-choked ravine. A few metres off the trail, walkers can peer down into its leafy depths.

Just a few minutes into this forest, traffic sounds fade, sunlight filters through branches overhead, and the aroma of earth and cedar fills the air. Lush ferns, salal, holly and salmonberry bushes line the trails. Spiders' webs glisten and mushrooms cluster on fallen trunks. An occasional woodpecker drums on rotting trees, and tiny wrens and juncos flit about. A chipmunk scurries down a Douglas fir and sometimes frogs serenade. Although raccoons, weasels, skunks,

otters and foxes make their homes in the undergrowth, they are usually shy when people are around.

Where the trail slopes down sharply and becomes rougher, it soon divides. The Spanish Trail heads steeply downhill

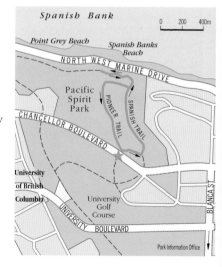

*and north to Spanish Banks Beach,
soon visible through the trees. The
Pioneer Trail turns west, through
a wooden gate.*

Climb over a fallen tree trunk to an
open glade called the Plains of
Abraham. At the turn of the 20th
century, a John Stewart ran a dairy
farm here, but the once-visible
foundations have now become
overgrown with fireweed and
blackberry bushes. A sign to the
southwest indicates the Pioneer Trail,
the corduroy road built by Stewart so
that he could haul his milk to market.

*For a longer walk, cross the western edge
of the clearing and follow the winding
trail north to the cliff edge, where it
swings west to run parallel to the clifftops
and provides views of Burrard Inlet and
the North Shore Mountains.*

The trail eventually ends at a clearing
on North West Marine Drive across
from the beach. Any blue herons flying
overhead are probably returning to
their homes hidden in these woods.

Some 33 trails meander 53km
(33 miles) through Pacific Spirit
Park, several beginning from the park
information office. All that is needed
is a map and a reasonable sense of
direction. Many are popular with dog
walkers, horse riders, joggers, hikers
and mountain bikers. Film makers
occasionally adapt the park for sets,
varying from the Amazon jungle
to rural Pennsylvania.

*The park is about a 20-minute drive
from downtown; count on half an hour
by bus (No 25). Maps are available at the
park information office on W 16th Ave
and at information boards at many
trailheads (contact GVRD Parks at
tel: (604) 224 5739).*

Rainforest at Pacific Spirit Park

Walk: Granville Island

Granville Island is actually a peninsula. Once a swampy, tidal flat and later the industrial heart of Vancouver, these 15 hectares (37 acres) of land are now an urban oasis of parks, walkways and renovated warehouses, popular for the many shops and galleries, restaurants and other diversions located here. (See www.granvilleisland.com)

Allow about 2 hours, plus extra time for more leisurely browsing and a meal.

Walk south from downtown for ten minutes to the foot of Hornby St or the Aquatic Centre and take the five-minute Aquabus mini-ferry ride across False Creek. There is complimentary three-hour parking for both cars and boats on the island, but places are extremely hard to find. It is much better to go on foot.

1 Arts Club theatres

Overlooking the ferry terminal are two Arts Club theatres. Walk right between them to the Information Centre which offers an audio-visual presentation on the evolution of the area.

Northwest is the Public Market, well worth a stroll through, if only to enjoy the aroma of a great array of local and imported food. On the waterfront, a bevy of buskers, including clowns and jugglers, entertain benches of visitors.

Northwest of the market is a good place to watch the yachts and motor-boats slip out to English Bay beyond. The deck at Bridges Restaurant (there may be a queue) is a super spot to sit in the sun or watch the sunset.
Turn south into Duranleau St.

2 Duranleau Street

Duranleau Street sports a series of maritime shops selling rugged outdoor wear, scuba gear, yacht fittings and other nautical equipment. Across the street, the Net Loft shelters a dozen shops, including Edie's Hats with a selection of stylish headgear; The Postcard Place; Paper Ya's which features handmade paper from around the world; Mesa, where a weaver may be at work at the loom; and the Wickaninnish Gallery of native jewellery and sculptures.
Cross Anderson St.

3 Granville Island Brewery

Across Anderson Street, the brewery produces a popular preservative-free light lager (Bavarian-style Pilsner), and offers free tastings every afternoon. *Cross over to Cartwright St.*

4 Cartwright Street

The Kids Only Market houses two dozen shops and activity areas, and a playcare centre for pre-schoolers. Just beyond the Waterfront Theatre is the supervised Water Park and the adjacent Cat's Meow restaurant, which has a children's play area inside. The rest of Cartwright Street is lined with art studios, galleries and craft shops. *Continue east to the Granville Island Hotel and the Sea Village.*

5 Sea Village

On the north shore, near a big, rusting crane overhead, is a fleet of floating homes, many with skylights and patios crowded with plants and flowers. The Sea Village is a private residential

NEARBY

Aquatic Centre, Waterfront Theatre

complex, but walk partway down the ramp to see a colourful collection of rural mailboxes. *Walk northwest along the boardwalk to the Emily Carr Institute of Art & Design.*

6 Emily Carr Institute of Art & Design

Here, big windows reveal students at work. Visitors are welcome to view the student art exhibits in the foyer. Beyond a few more craft shops along the shore is the ferry dock.

Active visitors can sign up for classes at the art studios, catch live music at the Arts Club Lounge, or go parasailing over English Bay. You can also rent a kayak to paddle up False Creek. *Return to the ferry.*

Walk: Granville Island

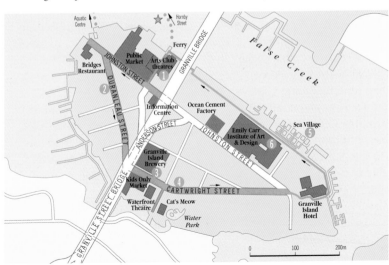

Vancouver Harbour

Vancouver Harbour is Canada's largest port and one of the top 20 in the world – the country's gateway to the Pacific Rim – and it plays a key role in international trade. Every year more than 3,000 ships, most flying foreign flags, carry bulk, general and containerised cargo between Vancouver and a hundred other ports around the world. The two dozen terminals circling Vancouver Harbour move more than 70 million tonnes of cargo annually. Enterprises engaged in this trade range from BC Sugar and United Grain Growers to Cassier Mining. For more information visit www.portvancouver.com

Beyond the Inner Harbour east of Second Narrows Bridge are several oil refineries and a major sulphur export operation at Port Moody. About 35km (22 miles) south of downtown, near the BC Ferries dock at Tsawwassen, the Westshore Terminals at Roberts Bank ship coal, sulphur and timber to other countries.

Canada Place Promenade

Canada Place has a wrap-around public promenade for observing the Inner Harbour. A self-directed walk, called 'Promenade into History', follows a series of plaques describing historical waterfront events. The promenade also provides great dockside viewing of some of the world's most luxurious cruise ships, which run from here to Alaska from May to September. Canada Place is home to the CN IMAX Theatre. *Tel: (604) 682 IMAX; www.imax.com*

Panoramic vantage points

Harbour-view rooms at the Pan Pacific, Waterfront Centre and Renaissance hotels enable visitors to Vancouver to get orientated quickly. Much cheaper are the bird's-eye vantage points at Vistas, the revolving restaurant atop the Renaissance Hotel, where visitors can enjoy regional specialities or coffee and dessert as the harbour panorama moves by.

The Lookout!, a circular observation deck high above Harbour Centre (*tel: (604) 689 0421*), also affords a 360-degree view of the harbour and the city, and photographic plaques and decorative display panels relate the history and character of the area. But there is an admission charge.

Views from the water

For a view of the harbour from the water, take the SeaBus (*tel: (604) 953 3333*) from the downtown terminal to

North Vancouver. Alternatively, contact any Travel InfoCentre (*tel: (604) 683 2000; www.tourismvancouver.com*) for details about harbour cruises.

Waterfront parks

Several parks around Burrard Inlet offer great picnic spots and harbour views. From the Stanley Park Port Look Out, on the seawall just south of Brockton Point, almost the whole harbour is visible, and a series of plaques outlines port operations.

Much smaller **Portside Park**, just east of Canada Place at the foot of Main Street, offers grassy slopes, children's play areas and a good view of various marine activities. **New Brighton Park**, further east and adjacent to the Alberta Wheat Pool just off McGill Street, has a pool (*tel: (604) 298 0222*), a pier, lots of open space, views of grain and forest products handling facilities and the ships sailing through the Second Narrows.

Waterfront Park, located between the Lonsdale Quay and the Pacific Marine Training Institute in North Vancouver, provides a panorama of the harbour and the city skyline. Harbour View Park, located further east on a narrow strip of land at the mouth of Lynn Creek, features a creek-side walking trail and a platform for observing the loading and unloading of forest products.

Vancouver's redeveloped False Creek

Harbour life

Vancouver is the largest port in Canada, providing the vital link with the Pacific Rim nations. It will come as no surprise, therefore, to discover that Vancouver Harbour was once almost exclusively industrial. However, this is no longer the case. Extensive development is underway, concentrated in three main areas, all of which are on the waterfront: Coal Harbour near Stanley Park; Yaletown where redevelopment is complete; and East False Creek near the Science Centre.

The development at Coal Harbour is one of the most extensive waterfront revitalisations in North America. Stretching east of Stanley Park to the Trade and Convention Centre at the foot of Burrard Street, the city's newest community comprises a marina, park, community centre, offices and retail development. A number of townhouses and residential towers offer upmarket living, a short ten-minute walk from downtown Vancouver. When complete, the development is

The redeveloped Coal Harbour

Vancouver is a busy port

some 1,000 residential units and 16,250sq m (175,000sq ft) of commercial space – completes the revitalisation of this erstwhile neglected harbour area.

The pace of life in that part of the harbour occupied by pleasure craft is gentle. Residents here usually find time to chat and are friendly to visitors. One resident, who has worked here aboard his floating electronic cottage/houseboat for 20 years, says the tides are for him the pulse of Mother Nature. If he were never to leave his home for a whole year, he would still travel over 5km (3 miles), since harbour tides advance and retreat as much as 4.5m (15ft) twice daily.

Canada geese paddle up to his houseboat most mornings for breakfast, while hunched blue herons stalk along the shore for snacks, and kingfishers dive for minnows. Loons and cormorants patrol the waters, along with ever-present shrieking seagulls. Starfish and mussels hug the pillars that keep the docks in place, while crabs crawl and feed along the bottom. Harbour seals occasionally watch from further offshore.

In winter, harbour dwellers can pull out binoculars and look up to Grouse Mountain across Burrard Inlet to see if there's still room for more skiers on the slopes. It's quite a lifestyle!

expected to cater to approximately 3,500 people.

In the 1980s Yaletown was the industrial backyard of downtown Vancouver, full of warehouses and light industry – it even had a sawmill. Today, while the distinctive stone-paved streets and many stone and brick buildings still remain, the warehouses have been replaced by trendy furniture showrooms and design studios. The streets are dotted with restaurants, nightclubs and coffee houses. Residential development in this now up-scale and popular area hugs the waterfront. The redevelopment along East False Creek – a cluster of towers offering

Tour: Boat ride on a bus

The SeaBus provides an inexpensive harbour cruise, along with a great opportunity to explore Lonsdale Quay and Waterfront Park in North Vancouver. The crossing takes 15 minutes.

Allow 2 hours.

Start the tour at the Waterfront Station, located at the end of Water St.

1 SeaBus Station

Tall, creamy pillars mark the entrance to this classic old brick building. The beautifully renovated interior of the terminal showcases a series of paintings from 1916 of the Rocky Mountains, looking down on a large lobby surrounded by several shops, fast-food stops and coffee bars.

Pause briefly on the overhead ramp en route to the SeaBus to watch railcars being shunted ahead and back over the shining rails, as trains load and unload. Then board the SeaBus for the sail across the inner harbour.

The SeaBuses, appropriately named the SS *Beaver* and the SS *Otter*, have no outside decks, but the windows provide a maritime artwork of freighters with many foreign flags, luxury cruise ships sailing to and from Alaska, a variety of smaller pleasure craft, and float planes taking off and landing. North looms the imposing majesty of the Coast Range, west the forest green peninsula of Stanley Park, and the Lions Gate Bridge. Southward stand the shining sails of Canada Place and the mirrored high-rises of downtown, in sharp contrast to an eastward-stretching line of old buildings huddled along the waterfront.

After disembarking on the North Shore, turn right to Lonsdale Quay.

2 Lonsdale Quay

The ground floor of this airy glass and steel structure, right at the water's edge, features a public market with a colourful assortment of local and imported fruit and vegetables, meat and fish, breads and pastries, cut and dried flowers and potted plants. Inexpensive fast-food restaurants serve everything from Italian pizza to Vietnamese salad rolls. A snack, a coffee or a cold drink on the outside deck includes the stunning harbour view. The second level has a charming collection of gift shops and boutiques, while the third level is the entrance to the Lonsdale Quay Hotel.

*West from the Quay and the SeaBus
Terminal lies Waterfront Park.*

3 Waterfront Park

A leisurely stroll along the meandering,
wide, paved walkway takes about half
an hour. Along the seawall, signs
identify prominent downtown
buildings. A short wooden pier with a
covered (it does rain here occasionally!)
observation deck and benches juts out
over the water. During the summer
months, musical concerts are held here
on many Sunday afternoons and, at
other times, local clubs enjoy kite-
flying, square dancing, vintage car
shows and native pow-wows. A
noticeboard at the west end of the park
lists events, dates and times.

Beside the walkway stands a huge
series of irregular, separate steel arches
spanning a shrub-covered gully, a

modernistic sculpture entitled
Cathedral by artist Douglas Senft. A
little further west, an elegant, stylised
sundial dominates Sailor's Point Plaza.
The base of the sculpture contains tiny
sketches of sunken ships. The plaza is
dedicated to people who have lost their
lives at sea in both peace and wartime.
A plaque on the plaza celebrates
Captain George Vancouver, the
European who discovered and named
Burrard Inlet.

Before heading back, peek through
the windows of the Pacific Marine
Training Institute to see the assembly of
nautical devices used by modern
mariners in training.

*The SeaBus runs every 15 to 30 minutes
from 6am to 6pm and at half-hour
intervals during the evening.
Tel: (604) 953 3333; www.translink.bc.ca*

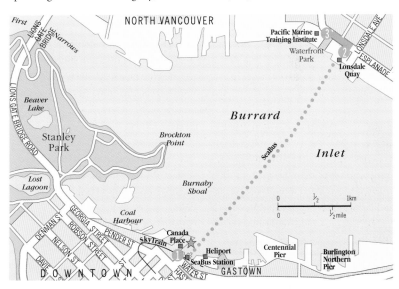

Historic houses

Vancouver, like Los Angeles, seems to have suffered from the philosophy of down with the old and up with the new, as far as preserving historic ('heritage') homes is concerned. But a few treasures remain.

The Mansion

This elegant Victorian stone mansion was built in 1900 by American sugar tycoon B T Rogers as a family residence. The original home had 18 fireplaces with self-cleaning flues (several of which remain), and a pantry cooled by ice. The walls are oak-panelled, and the floors laid with teak from Fiji. A spectacular stained-glass window overlooks the staircase which rises from the main foyer. It depicts three women believed to represent the virtues of faith, hope and charity, and the graces of wisdom, youth and beauty. The background is decked with BC wild flowers and seashells.

Other features of the house include a walk-in humidor for cigar smokers and, outside, a wrought-iron fence built from balconies of the old San Francisco City Hall. It now houses an Italian restaurant called Romano's Macaroni Grill, noted for its good pasta, which is open for both lunch and dinner. *1523 Davie St, a five-minute walk from English Bay. Tel: (604) 689 4334.*

Irving House

'The handsomest, the best and most home-like house of which BC can yet boast' was the 1865 newspaper description of this 14-room home, which originally belonged to 'King of the River' Captain William Irving. The small parlour and master bedroom contain Irving's furniture, including a red rocking chair from a Fraser River

The Mansion

sternwheeler, a piano shipped round Cape Horn in 1858 and a black horsehair settee transported across the plains from Missouri. The kitchen features a classic black and chrome pioneer stove laden with cast-iron pots and flat irons, and a hand-pumped vacuum cleaner. The kitchen floor was laid and caulked like the deck of a ship. The nursery upstairs contains a collection of dolls from the 19th century. In the library are a roll-top desk, a smoking table, a pump organ, a 17th-century grandfather clock and some fine Indian baskets.

302 Royal Ave, New Westminster. Tel: (604) 527 4640. Open: Wed–Sun noon–5pm (to 4pm Sept–Apr). Admission by donation.

Roedde House

Built in 1893 by the German immigrant Gustav Roedde, Vancouver's first bookbinder, this house is part of a park site that includes nine Victorian West End houses, most of them renovated for family accommodation.

Designed by F M Rattenbury, the architect responsible for the Empress Hotel, Roedde House is built in simple Queen Anne style, with a cupola, bay windows, an upstairs porch and a downstairs veranda. The interior has been furnished with period furniture to reflect city life at the turn of the 20th century.

1415 Barclay St, a ten-minute walk from the city centre. Tel: (604) 684 7040; www.roeddehouse.org. Guided tours

The Victorian façade of Roedde House

Tue–Sat 10am–4pm, Sun 2–4pm; group tours by appointment. Admission charge.

Le Gavroche

A good way to make the past present is by enjoying a meal in a heritage home restaurant. Named after the street urchin in *Les Misérables*, Le Gavroche was established in 1979 in a refurbished three-storey Victorian house whose roof is green with moss, looking out to the Bayshore Hotel and Coal Harbour. The intimate, dimly-lit interior, with its oak floors, flickering flames in the wood-burning fireplace, and dark floral-print wallpaper contrasting with white tablecloths, quickly transports diners back to a more romantic time. The restaurant is renowned for refined service, fine French cuisine and one of the city's best wine collections.

1616 Alberni St. Tel: (604) 685 3924; www.legavroche.com

Museums

A wide variety of city museums provides an in-depth look at the history and cultural life of Vancouver and BC, with exhibits ranging from food and maritime history to sports and First Nations cultures.

Museum of Anthropology

The Museum of Anthropology at the University of British Columbia, probably Canada's most memorable museum, is best known for its superb collection of art and artefacts of the province's First Nations peoples. The spectacular concrete-and-glass structure sits on a cliff overlooking English Bay and, beyond, the North Shore Mountains and Howe Sound. Inside the MOA, as it is affectionately called, a dozen galleries house a great variety of objects, which express the complex social and ceremonial life of many cultures from around the world.

Entrance to the World of Art

The museum's cedar entrance doors, designed and carved by contemporary Ksan master carvers, depict the joining of heaven and earth in the creation of the first Gitksan people. The doors, along with the adjoining side panels, form a rectangular structure inspired by the traditional Indian bent box.

Carvings from traditional West Coast house interiors, with illustrations showing their original placement, border the entrance ramp. At the base of the ramp, a bear sculpted by the contemporary artist Bill Reid, of the Haida people, is one of the few touchable exhibits in the museum. Be sure to feel its square snout and large teeth, nostrils and ears, characteristic of Haida bear carvings.

The spectacular Great Hall

In the Great Hall, natural light streams through 14m (46ft) high windows,

Haida carvings

which illuminate an exquisite assembly of weathered cedar totem poles. Totem poles do not usually tell a story, but depict creatures representing the genealogy of the families that raised them. Ravens, bears, beavers, frogs, eagles and wolves are often an integral part of tribal crests. Totem poles have traditionally been raised to identify families or to commemorate the departed, and a raising continues to be an occasion for a *potlatch*, or celebration. A selection of red cedar chests, carved canoes and dishes complements the display.

The Museum of Anthropology displays a fine collection of Northwest Coast Indian art

Highlights of the galleries

The Masterpiece Gallery houses an intriguing collection of intricately carved miniatures in silver, gold, argillite, ivory, bone, horn and wood, mostly dating from the 19th century.

But the highlight of the contemporary collection is the acclaimed sculpture *The Raven and the First Men*, carved in laminated yellow cedar by Bill Reid, and displayed in a skylighted rotunda. The sculpture is a dramatic portrayal of the birth of mankind, with the first Haida people emerging both frontwards and backwards from a partially open clam shell (*see p38*).

Behind this sculpture, several cases display 30 of Reid's smaller carvings in cedar, boxwood and argillite, along with some gold and silver jewellery pieces. These works span 40 years of creative activity, from early explorations in Haida design to his distinctive, mature style, now recognised around the world.

The Research Collections, since the museum is both a public and a teaching institution, feature a visible storage system, with a series of glass-covered drawers and cases that let visitors see but not touch more than 10,000 objects, arranged in cultural and artefact categories.

The outdoor exhibits

One of the best exhibits is outdoors on the grassy area between the museum and the cliff. The Kwakiutl, Haida and Gitksan totem poles standing here with two Haida houses, one for the living and one for the dead, are completely at one with nature.

On the UBC campus at 6393 Northwest Marine Drive. Tel: (604) 822 3825; www.moa.ubc.ca. Open: summer daily 10am–5pm (9pm on Tue); winter Wed–Sun 11am–5pm (9pm on Tue). Closed: Mon. Admission charge, except Tue evenings.

BC Golf Museum

A collection of golf memorabilia to delight the enthusiastic golfer.
2545 Blanca St. Tel: (604) 222 4653; www.bcgolfmuseum.org. Open: Tue–Sun noon–4pm.

BC Sports Hall of Fame and Museum

This museum provides high-tech, hands-on sports entertainment. Visitors can run, throw, climb and row their way through the computer-enhanced Hall of Champions which honours BC's elite athletes and teams, or test their athletic skills against top competitors in the Participation Gallery. The museum covers 150 years of history, from 1850s Native games to videos of recent sporting events.
At BC Place Stadium. Tel: (604) 687 5520; www.bcsportshalloffame.com. Open: daily 10am–5pm. Admission charge.

Canadian Museum of Flight

This outdoor assembly of vintage aircraft includes bombers, biplanes, jets and helicopters. The museum also has a picnic area and playground for children.
Hanger 3, 5333-216 St, Langley. Tel: (604) 532 0035; www.canadianflight.org. Open: daily 10am–4pm. Admission charge.

Granville Island Model Trains Museum

Kids and train fanatics alike enjoy the huge collection of model and toy trains

CAPTAIN GEORGE VANCOUVER

George Vancouver, an English youth of Dutch descent, joined the British navy at the age of 13, and went on to serve Captain Cook on his second and third voyages. In 1791, Captain Vancouver set out from England aboard HMS *Discovery*, sailed south around the Cape of Good Hope, and a year later reached the northern Pacific coast of North America. He had been tasked to survey the coast and negotiate a land settlement with Spanish Captain Bodega y Quadra, at Nootka, on what is now known as Vancouver Island.

Without realising that the Spaniards had charted this region before him, Vancouver claimed all the land he saw for King George III.

Vancouver returned to England in 1795 and died three years later aged 40. Spain, after the Mexican revolution, eventually abandoned all claims to the Pacific Northwest.

– said to be the world's largest such collection on display.
1502 Duranleau St. Tel: (604) 483 1939; www.modeltrainsmuseum.ca. Open: Tue–Sun 10am–5.30pm. Admission charge.

H R MacMillan Space Centre

Multimedia astronomy shows, including special shows for children, and Canada's best laser light show, beamed on to a 20m (66ft) dome, bring the cosmos within reach. The cosmic Courtyard interactive gallery puts visitors at the controls. There is also a variety of special presentations in the GroundStation Canada mission control theatre, and exciting simulated journeys through space. The centre also has

some authentic space artefacts to see and a real moon rock to touch.
1100 Chestnut St, Vanier Park. Tel: (604) 738-STAR (7827); www.hrmacmillanspacecentre.com. Open: Tue–Sun 10am–5pm, and holidays; (daily in July & Aug). Admission charge.

Vancouver Maritime Museum

This museum explores the maritime world, with exciting tales of the sea and hands-on activities in its Children's Maritime Discovery Centre. There is a huge collection of model ships and many special exhibitions. The museum is home to the *St Roch*, a two-masted schooner which is now a National Historic Site. Built in the 1920s, it became the first ship to navigate

through the treacherous waters of the Northwest Passage.
1905 Ogden Ave. Tel: (604) 257 8300; www.vmm.bc.ca. Open: summer daily 10am–5pm; winter Tue–Sat 10am–5pm, Sun noon–5pm. Closed: Mon & Christmas Day. Tours available. Admission charge.

Vancouver Museum

This museum, which houses one of the largest civic collections in Canada, is devoted to regional history and the First Nations, but also features exhibitions of decorative arts from all over the world.
1100 Chestnut St. Tel: (604) 736 4431. Open: daily 10am–5pm; Thur 10am–9pm. Closed Mon Sept–June. Admission charge.

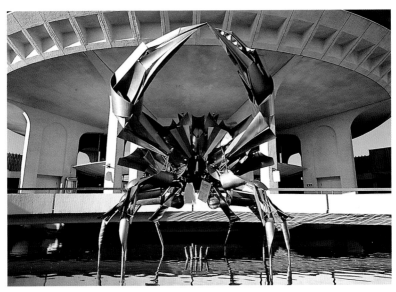

Crab sculpture at the H R MacMillan Space Centre

On the totem trail

At least 8,000 years ago, Asian peoples who lived by hunting and gathering berries crossed the icy land bridge that is now the Bering Strait and drifted south along the Pacific coast of North America and into the interior. When the Europeans arrived in the late 18th century, an estimated 80,000 of these native 'Indians' were living in what is now known as BC. Within a century, however, two-thirds of them had died from imported diseases.

Today, there are once again about 80,000 people of native Indian ancestry living in BC. The Salish inhabit the southwest of the province (the Lower Mainland) and the southeastern part of Vancouver Island. On the west coast of Vancouver Island are the Nootka. Further north along the coast reside the Kwakiutl, Bella Coola, Tsimshian, Haida and Tlingit peoples. Almost 80 per cent of BC's land area is subject to 22 native land claims,

The exquisite artistry of the Northwest Coast Indian totem poles in Vancouver's Stanley Park

Totem poles are heavy with symbolism

including most of greater Vancouver. The struggle to regain self-esteem and self-reliance has been accelerating. There has been a visible renaissance in the arts, in totem poles, masks, talking sticks, bent boxes, canoes, clothing and jewellery.

Totem poles, the largest wood-carvings known, are scattered throughout Vancouver. Some of the best are in Stanley Park, at the Museum of Anthropology and at the Capilano Suspension Bridge (*www.capbridge.com*). Carving of totem poles can be viewed at The Big House at Capilano Suspension Bridge. Some of these carved cedar poles are memorials to the dead, others portray family trees, while still others relate mythological adventures.

Carved in a stylised realism, totem poles are sometimes difficult to decipher, but here are some of the creatures commonly seen. The thunderbird is the creator and controller of all elements and spirits. The raven is credited with providing light, fire and water. The whale symbolises strength and bravery. The bear, regarded as an elder kinsman, represents strength, authority and mobility. The eagle represents wisdom, authority and power, and the salmon abundance and prosperity.

The Orpheum: a Canadian classic

Here, in one of North America's youngest cities, the patina of the past so prevalent in Europe is most wonderfully preserved in the Orpheum Theatre. This gracious old building boasts a history of hosting such great artists as Charlie Chaplin, Igor Stravinsky and Helen Hayes. Its grand opening in 1927 was a social highlight in city history. The Orpheum, with 2,800 seats, was then the largest theatre on the Pacific coast. The premiere featured a silent movie, but people really came to see the vaudeville: Marie White and the Blue Slickers, dance exponents Chaney and Fox, Ethel Davis in refreshing song chatter, and everybody's favourite, Toto the clown with his little dog, Whiskey.

Interior and backstage wonders

The Orpheum has always been a star, even with mediocre performers. Originally built as a link in the Chicago-based theatre chain, it was designed in conservative Spanish Renaissance style, with a basic colour scheme of antique ivory and gold. Ornamented pilasters and colonnades, highlighted with imitation and sometimes real gold leaf, contrasted with rich tapestries of black and gold arabesques, creating an aura of exotic luxury. Dramatic maroon velvet draperies lent a regal touch. A hundred glittering chandeliers lit the hall.

Beneath the stage, an electrically operated mechanism raised and lowered three big Wurlitzer organs, which sounded like a full orchestra.

One is still played a few times every year. An animal room accommodated the assortment of dogs, monkeys, tigers and elephants featured in some of the

VANCOUVER SYMPHONY ORCHESTRA

The historic Orpheum Theatre has been home to the Vancouver Symphony Orchestra since 1930. Each year, apart from a full concert season extending from October to April, the orchestra presents special outdoor concerts around the region in summer. In September 2000, Bramwell Tovey became Music Director. Also gifted as an orator, Tovey gives regular lectures on forthcoming programmes an hour before the performance starts – arrive an hour early in order to avail yourself of this opportunity.
*601 Smythe St. Tel: (604) 876 3434; www.vancouversymphony.ca.
Concert tickets are available online at www.ticketmaster.ca*

shows. An efficient ventilation system changed the air in the theatre every three minutes. One Orpheum manager said the downstairs was spooky and uncomfortably reminiscent of *The Phantom of the Opera.*

Famous players and the talkies

During the early 1930s, when live music faded and talking pictures took over, the Orpheum passed into the hands of Famous Players Theatres. The Nabob Company sponsored elegant afternoon teas on the mezzanine.

One of the Orpheum's proudest moments was probably the Canadian premiere of *Gone With The Wind* in 1939. The theatre has attracted countless famous faces, including Marilyn Monroe, who came in 1956 to publicise *Gentlemen Prefer Blondes.*

Snack-vending machines appeared in the Orpheum in 1942, and a confectionery counter in 1945. By 1950, usherettes were selling confections from trays in the auditorium. From 1943 to 1954, Nabob's Harmony House was broadcast from coast to coast from 'Canada's most beautiful theatre'. One of the last *grandes premières* was *King Rat* in 1965, with a guest appearance by

Inside the Orpheum

author James Clavell, then living in West Vancouver.

Meanwhile, the Vancouver Symphony Orchestra had been a frequent performer from the early 1930s.

Restoration to former glory

In 1973, Famous Players announced that the Orpheum would be gutted to create six mini-cinemas, reflecting a continuing trend towards smaller theatres. Vancouverites wrote 8,500 letters in protest. Consequently, the city purchased the Orpheum for $3.9 million, and spent almost as much restoring the acoustics and fine furnishings. Octogenarian artist and decorator Tony Heinsbergen, who had worked on the original structure in 1927, supervised the interior decoration and painted the mural on the massive 20m (66ft) dome. Florentine Joseph Tinucci did much of the ornate and decorative plasterwork, and reproduced the columns that are now part of the soundshell.

In 1977, the Orpheum reopened, once again a breathtaking beauty and the finest heritage concert hall in the country. In 1983, a new foyer was completed, and the Orpheum was declared a National Historic Site. Today, the Orpheum is home to the Vancouver Symphony Orchestra and the BC Entertainment Hall of Fame.
884 Granville, Smythe St at Seymour.
Tel: (604) 665 3050;
www.city.vancouver.bc.ca/theatres.
Tours on request (charge).

The Orpheum: a Canadian classic

Places of worship

There are dozens of places of worship in Vancouver, thanks to the variety of visitors from all over the world who have settled here. The following are a few that might be of interest to anyone, regardless of creed. A listing of churches is found in the Practical Guide section on pp184–5.

Buddhist Temple

This temple is an exquisite example of Chinese palatial architecture, with gilded porcelain tiles and flying rooftop dragons. The interior is an artistic showcase of oriental sculpture, painting, carpentry and embroidery. An outdoor courtyard encloses a beautiful collection of bonsai plants and a ceramic mural of Kuan-Yin-Bodhisattva.

A 30-minute drive south from downtown; turn west at the exit by Fantasy Gardens towards Steveston. 9160 Steveston Highway, Richmond. Tel: (604) 274 2822; www.buddhisttemple.ca. Open: daily 9.30am–5.30pm. Free admission.

Canadian Memorial Church

Shortly after World War I, Chaplain George Fallis came to Vancouver with the idea of building a memorial to Canadians who had served in the war. He found a congregation with the same idea, solicited the support of local leaders, and then headed east across Canada to find further funding. The result was the Canadian Memorial Church, which opened in 1928 at the 11th hour of the 11th day of the 11th month – mortgage-free.

The church is constructed in greystone Gothic-style. The main attraction is the stained-glass windows, each of which depicts a biblical scene. The provincial coats of arms beneath are flanked by historical illustrations.

The BC window depicts a soldier's faith, with Christ meeting a Roman centurion pleading on behalf of his palsied servant. The historic panels show Captain Vancouver at Nootka Sound in 1792 and Simon Fraser exploring the Fraser River in 1808.

The Nova Scotia window illustrates the arrival of Jacques Cartier in 1543 and of Lord Rollo, the first Englishman, in 1759. The Yukon window depicts the Chilkoot Pass in 1898 and a Royal Mail dog team with carriole.

The spectacular chancel window portrays a biblical motif of sacrifice and young manhood. The all-Canada window facing north depicts the services rendered by all men and women of Canada throughout World War I.

The windows are interesting for their comments on world peace and history and for their exquisite craftsmanship. *At the southwest corner of Burrard St & 15th Ave. Tel: (604) 731 3101; www.canadianmemorial.org.*
Open: regular church services are held on Sun morning at 10.30am, but for many visitors who may prefer to study the windows in relative solitude, staff at the community centre, adjacent to the church

on 16th Ave, keep the keys and escort those interested to the chapel during regular business hours.

Christ Church Cathedral

Located in the heart of downtown Vancouver, this century-old sanctuary looks as though it should be nestled into a green valley in rural England. Of special interest are the English and Canadian stained-glass windows, and a tableau of the Crucifixion.
690 Burrard St. Tel: (604) 682 3848; www.cathedral.vancouver.bc.ca.
Open: Mon–Fri 9.30am–4pm.
Free admission.

Westminster Abbey

This modern Benedictine monastery is both a high school and a degree-granting theological seminary. Every Sunday the ten bells of the 50m (164ft) tower chime over the valley to announce Mass. Resident monks create and restore paintings and other forms of art in an atmosphere of peace and tranquillity. Various sculptures, stained-glass windows and murals decorate the monastery. Overnight rooms are available (reservations recommended), as St Benedict believed that there should always be guests at a monastery.
34224 Dewdney Trunk Rd, near the town of Mission, an hour's drive east from Vancouver. Tel: (604) 826 8975.
Open: Mon–Fri 1.30–4pm; Sun 2–4pm. Guided tours available. Modest dress requested. Donations accepted.

A corner of the garden at the Buddhist Temple

Places of worship

Science World

A hundred years ago, the site of Science World was a swamp covered with water. Today, its silver geodesic sphere is a city landmark, shimmering over the eastern end of False Creek. Billed as the most curious place on earth, this science complex attracts 500,000 inquiring minds a year. Most visitors like to spend two to three hours at Science World, and many enjoy lunch or a snack before moving on. The street-level foyer houses the Information Centre, cloakrooms, telephones and an interesting gift shop.

Scientific wonders discovered

Our World focuses on the challenges and solutions of creating a sustainable future. The exhibit addresses real world issues including transportation, electricity, water consumption, garbage/waste disposal and food production.

In the Eureka! Gallery on the second level, visitors can learn about everything from potential energy to sound through bright, engaging exhibits and games. The nearby Search Gallery focuses on the natural history of BC. There are tree roots hanging from the ceiling, a crawl-through beaver lodge, a hollow tree and a see-through beehive.

Bodyworks offers interactive exhibits that investigate individual strength, endurance, speed, reaction time, dexterity, accuracy, memory and much more. The science behind human performance and the relationship between athletic and everyday activities are the focus of this new exhibition.

In the Feature Gallery, interactive exhibits which change regularly might include kaleidoscopes; challenging puzzles with tangrams (Chinese puzzles which consist of several basic shapes which can be combined to form a great variety of other figures) and geometric shapes; and the study of physiognomy, in which the curious can observe how faces express feeling, deceive, encode identity and record experiences.

Big-screen excitement

The third level houses the 400-seat OMNIMAX Theatre (the screen is 27m/89ft wide), where the audience is surrounded with awesome images on one of the world's largest domed screens and engulfed in wrap-around sound. These larger-than-life shows may cover such subjects as the origin of the universe, life above and below the ocean, and the explosive ring of fire circling the Pacific Rim.

Dazzling demonstrations

Science World presents audience participation shows daily at Centre Stage. These lively and entertaining programmes focus on such diverse subjects as bubbles, balance, kinetic engineering and liquid nitrogen. Designed to keep youngsters in touch with discoveries in science and technology, and its expanding frontier, Science World organises special events for children from time to time.

1455 Quebec St, across from the Main St SkyTrain station.
Tel: (604) 443 7443;
www.scienceworld.bc.ca.
Open: daily 10am–6pm.
Admission charge.

Science World

The futuristic Science World is a spectacular city landmark

Stanley Park

In a province as vast and varied as BC, there are many close-to-nature hideaways. But it is relatively rare to find an urban wilderness so accessible to so many people as Stanley Park. About a ten-minute walk from downtown, the park covers an area of 400 hectares (988 acres, about the same size as Central Park in New York City), jutting northward into Burrard Inlet and marking the entrance to Vancouver Harbour. Surrounding it is a 10km (6-mile) seawall popular with walkers, cyclists and rollerbladers.

From wilderness to park

Remarkable foresight on the part of Vancouver's city council in 1886 resulted in the creation of Stanley Park. The swampy peninsula was then a naval reserve where deer, bear, raccoon and cougar roamed along narrow trails and abandoned logging roads. The council petitioned the federal government to set it aside as a park.

The petition was granted, leaving only Deadman's Island as a naval base. So in 1888, the then Governor General of Canada, Lord Stanley, dedicated the park 'to the use and enjoyment of people of all colours, creeds and customs for all time'.

A park for all tastes

Today, about 8 million people a year come from all over Canada and the world to enjoy Stanley Park. Even on a warm summer day, visitors who do not want to mingle with the crowds can seek out the solitude of a shady trail.

Stanley Park is many things to many people. To youngsters, it is the sandy beach, a baby beluga whale, or a miniature railway. To teenagers, it is a trysting place and a playground for such sports as football (soccer), skateboarding, rollerblading and cycling.

To families, the park often means a leisurely Sunday picnic on a blanket under weeping willows. To the many elderly who live nearby in the West End concrete jungle, this urban oasis provides access to nature and the opportunity for a pleasant stroll around Lost Lagoon to feed the birds and squirrels.

Recovery and restoration

This once-dense park-forest was hit by a devastating storm in December 2006. An estimated 10,000 trees were lost, and popular trails became unusable. The city is committed to the restoration and reforestation of the park. Stanley Park's improvements will include the reinforcement and

The Teahouse, Stanley Park

rebuilding of seawalls, road and trail repair, and the establishment of environmental art projects.

Park wildlife

There are few wild animals in the park today, except for the sealife in the aquarium, and the squirrels, raccoons and skunks around Lost Lagoon. Occasionally, a black-tailed deer swims over from the North Shore to enjoy a free lunch. The last cougar disappeared nearly 50 years ago.

The beavers have been removed from Beaver Lake, because their efficient sawmill and logging operations were destroying many trees and leaving others to fall on unsuspecting visitors. They also dug tunnels that undermined the miniature railway and penetrated the bison pen. After Easter every year, a suspicious number of domestic bunnies appear in the park, suggesting that some parents have given their children more than they can handle.

It was migratory birds, however, that introduced carp to the Lost Lagoon, named by poetess Pauline Johnson because its waters used to disappear at low tide. The water, now locked in by man-made devices, is fresh. The Lost Lagoon area is a bird sanctuary, home to cormorants, mergansers, scaup, ringbill, green wing-tail, shovelers, mallard and many other species of feathered friends.

A few hundred Canada geese also maintain residence here, and another thousand or so fly in for the winter. In spring, mother geese, ducks and swans parade proudly around with gaggles of young ones.

Bald eagles, which have several nests in the park, fly over Lost Lagoon and, on occasions, shamelessly grab an unsuspecting mallard for a meal, totally indifferent to horrified onlookers who have forgotten that Mother Nature is both creative and cruel.

Stanley Park attractions

Shortly after the park opened in 1889, the warden adopted a black bear, which he kept tethered to a tree stump. Apparently, the local vicar's wife used to bring over household scraps to feed the bear. But one day the bear ignored the food and took a swipe at the lady's skirt. He was then banished to a bear pit, and it was decided to set aside an enclosed section of the park for wild animals.

The zoo grew to house 400 animals representing 90 different species. However, it was shut down because people were concerned about the relatively small area the animals had to live in. All that remains is the Children's Farmyard, which affords a great opportunity for youngsters to hug and be nuzzled by dozens of domestic animals. As well as the usual rabbits and goats, this 'petting zoo' includes such unusual species as Jacob sheep, Vietnamese pot-bellied pigs and miniature cows, along with various reptiles and birds.

To see wild animals, visitors must now drive an hour east from downtown to the Greater Vancouver Zoo (*tel: (604) 856 6825*), where giraffes, lions, tigers, camels, hippos and 100 other species roam a rangeland of 48 hectares (119 acres).

The Stanley Park Miniature Railway, which partly owes its existence to the terrific winds that uprooted thousands of trees and created an open area in the 1960s, has always carried more adults than children. Passengers ride in little canopied coaches pulled by a replica of the engine that led the first trans-continental train in to Vancouver in 1887. The ten-minute ride along the narrow rails goes through an avalanche tunnel and round a small artificial lake. *Tel: (604) 257 8531. Open: Feb–Sept 10am–5pm; Oct–Jan Sat–Sun 11am–4pm. Admission charge.*

Vancouver Aquarium

The Vancouver Aquarium is home to more than 9,000 aquatic creatures. A 5.5m (18ft) high bronze sculpture of a leaping killer whale, expertly crafted by Haida artist Bill Reid, marks the entrance.

Inside the aquarium, the more active denizens of the deep range from delicate seahorses to smiling crocodiles. Killer whales are no longer on display. The Marine Mammal Deck is a great viewing place. A wall-size viewing window shows playful sea otters cavorting above and below water. On the same deck is another area for harbour seals.

The Arctic Canada exhibition lets visitors look beneath the polar ice of the High Arctic at graceful white beluga whales; the big underwater windows make for excellent viewing.

Other sights and sounds of the far north, including fish with antifreeze genetically built in, are presented in a discovery centre within the aquarium.

The North Pacific Gallery and the Rufe Gibbs Hall have displays of such Canadian coastal water residents as giant octopuses, silvery salmon and waving sea anemones.

The humid Amazon Gallery provides pathways for strolling through a small tropical jungle, with banana and other equatorial trees where sloths hang lazily

White beluga whales never fail to draw attention at the Vancouver Aquarium

in the heat. Brightly coloured tropical birds flit among the tiny marmosets living in treetops, while in the water, other imported Amazon residents include anacondas, piranhas, stingrays and electric eels.

The Tropical Gallery features steely-eyed sharks, fish that glow in the dark, and rainbows of reef fishes whose families come from the clear blue waters of the Caribbean and Australia's Great Barrier Reef.

Children especially enjoy the tidal pools where they can touch anemones, chitons and starfish. School children frequently tour the zoo and aquarium on weekday mornings, so the afternoon is usually a less crowded time to visit.

The aquarium's Summer Speakers Series offers early evening lectures by naturalists on a variety of topics, and there are daily Dive Shows and Meet the Trainer talks.

Stanley Park Aquarium. Tel: (604) 659 3521. Open: daily, summer 9.30am–7pm; winter 9.30am–5pm. Admission charge. Aquarium: www.vanaqua.org

A statue of the orca killer whale, no longer seen live at the Aquarium

By bike: The seawall

The Stanley Park Seawall must be one of the best urban cycle routes in the world. About 150 benches line the seawall. Several shops near the Georgia Street entrance to the park, a ten-minute walk from most downtown hotels, hire bicycles and tandems by the hour. The 10km (6-mile) long paved pathway follows the perimeter of the 400-hectare (988-acre) peninsular park. The right side of the pathway, which is mostly level, is set aside for cyclists and rollerbladers. The trail runs anticlockwise and begins at Lost Lagoon. Walk bikes along the underpass and right to the seawall.

Allow about 2 hours.

1 Vancouver Rowing Club

Just past the Km 0 sign is the Tudor-style Vancouver Rowing Club. Single sculls and eights skim Coal Harbour's sheltered waters where coal was discovered in the 1800s. Across the harbour, the city skyline is highlighted by the big white canvas sails of Canada Place. Almost opposite the Rowing Club stands a statue of Lord Stanley, a former Governor General of Canada who, in 1889, dedicated the park 'to the use and enjoyment of people of all colours, creeds and customs for all time'.

2 Nine O'Clock Gun

A little further along stands a statue of Scottish poet Robert Burns and another of Harry Jerome, once the world's fastest runner. The Nine O'Clock Gun, which once called herring fishermen home, still booms every evening.

3 Brockton Point

A bright red-and-white-striped lighthouse marks Brockton Point, where fishermen cast their lines. Across Burrard Inlet brilliant yellow piles of sulphur await export. Behind lies Brockton Oval, a cinder jogging track encircling a summer cricket pitch which is used by rugby players in winter. A little further along, the bronze sculpture of *Girl in a Wet Suit* sits in the water near the shore, set against the Lions Gate Bridge.

4 Lumberman's Arch

At Lumberman's Arch, near Km 3, grassy slopes overlook a water park for children. This was once the site of a Squamish native village, and tons of seashells from the midden were used to surface the first road in the park in 1888. It is a short cycle off the seawall to the aquarium and zoo (*see pp72–3*).

5 Prospect Point

Prospect Point is the highest point in the park, where a cairn commemorates the SS *Beaver*, the pioneer steamship of the Pacific that sank nearby in 1888. You can see the huge pillars that support the Lions Gate Bridge.

6 Siwash Rock

A little further on, Siwash Rock juts defiantly skyward from the sea. The rock is the subject of an Indian legend. Millennia ago, a handsome young chief and his wife lived nearby. When their son was born the chief plunged into the waters to cleanse himself to ensure a spotless life for the newborn. At that moment giants in a canoe demanded that the chief forsake this ritual bath and go ashore. He refused, and they were so impressed by his love and devotion to the child, that they transformed him into Siwash Rock, to stand forever as a monument to Clean Fatherhood. The legend was recorded a century ago by Mohawk poet-princess Pauline Johnson, who is buried in a leafy glade nearby.

7 Second Beach

Second Beach has a popular children's playground and a sandy beach. The cycle trail crosses the main road through the park, and passes a Japanese-style bridge crossing a willow-banked stream. Beyond are a pitch-and-putt golf course, lawn bowling greens, tennis courts and a fine Mediterranean-style restaurant.

The trail continues over a humped bridge and follows the southern shore along Lost Lagoon to the start of the tour.

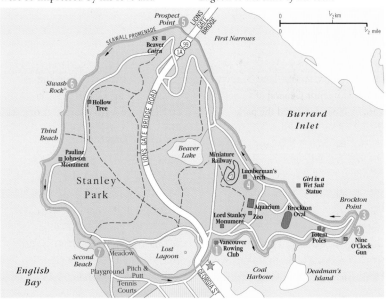

Unknown Vancouver

Although Vancouverites love their city, they sometimes take local treasures for granted, so visitors have to hunt to find them. Such local newspapers as the *Georgia Strait*, along with local radio and television stations, provide information on the area's life and leisure. Almost every weekend sees a variety of community events. In winter there's the Lantern Procession at Hastings Park, while summer brings Theater Under the Stars – outdoor theatre in Stanley Park – and the Point Grey Sandcastle Festival. Libraries often hold readings by Canadian authors, and visitors may purchase a temporary card to borrow books.

For an outdoor adventure, try picking strawberries, raspberries and blueberries in the Fraser Valley during the summer months. Salmonberries and blackberries can also be picked along many country roads and trails.

A great way to see the suburbs is to take in a garage sale. Local community newspapers list the sale venues. It is interesting to see what is sold and bought. People are very rarely in a hurry. It is, therefore, easy to strike up conversations. And you may get your Christmas shopping done early and at reduced prices.

Capilano Salmon Hatchery

Here you can watch salmon in various stages of growth in glass-fronted holding tanks. In the spawning season, the fish swim upstream and leap ladders into the hatchery.
4500 Capilano Park Rd, off Capilano Rd, in North Vancouver. Tel: (604) 666 1790. Open: daily 8am–4pm; until 7 or 8pm in the summer. Free admission.

Cultus Lake

Golfers and watersports fans can head out to Cultus Lake, the home of Lindell Beach Holiday Resort. The resort offers fully equipped holiday rental homes, perfect for self-catering travellers. There's a lakeside beach, a pool and a variety of activities.
Just outside Cultus Lake on Columbia Valley Road. Tel: (604) 484 0984, freephone (866) 369 6100.

Vancouver Flea Market

Bargain shopping is a favourite pastime in Vancouver, and the flea market is a mecca for junk-hunters. At this event, both junk and genuine bargains fill the display tables.
703 Terminal Ave, close to the Main St SkyTrain. Tel: (604) 685 0666. Open: Sat, Sun and hols 10am–5pm.

Yaletown

Yaletown, the trendiest downtown area, centres around Mainland Street between Nelson and Davie streets. Just over a century ago, this neighbourhood was rainforest wilderness – until 1887, when the Canadian Pacific Railway moved its operations from the little town of Yale to this spot on the north shore of False Creek. A shanty town of wood-frame homes, boarding houses and hotels developed here. One of the original wooden homes, the Perry Linden House, still stands at 1021 Richards Street.

From the early 20th century, brick warehouses replaced the wooden structures. By the 1950s, most residents had moved to the suburbs. In recent years, creative people have been converting the old warehouses into work and retail space, resulting in wonderful walking streets lined with shops, galleries and restaurants.

The growing selection of stores specialises in art supplies, coffee, flowers, designer and discounted clothing, sports and legal attire, and pricey home furnishings.

The Yaletown Galleria, at 1080 Mainland, houses three floors of offices and shops overlooking a central atrium. It's home to showrooms for antiques, furniture and accessories ranging from oriental urns to the latest in interior modern design. Drop in to Design House at 1080 Mainland to see how chic Vancouverites are furnishing their flats, or Global Atomic Design at 1006 Mainland for the latest in street fashion.

Mangiamo (*1116 Mainland; tel: (604) 687 1116*), recently voted one of Vancouver's favourite restaurants, features both Italian cuisine and décor. Cambie Street offers half a dozen interesting art galleries and Granville Island has speciality shops such as Maiwa Handprints, a fibre arts store.

Yaletown is not too glossy yet, although chic condos are sprouting around its perimeter. It is the kind of place where an advertising executive in a Gucci jacket might carry work home in a dustbin bag. Enjoy it quickly, before it changes.

For more information see *www.yaletowninfo.com*

Boulangerie on Mainland

Vancouver suburbs

Vancouver's outlying neighbourhoods have their own distinctive character. Visit Richmond for authentic Chinese restaurants and Hong Kong-style shopping. West Vancouver is the city's close-in, upscale neighbourhood, with lush gardens and opulent homes. Rapidly growing Surrey still maintains its historic character in the traditional farms and heritage parks. Many of the neighbourhoods can be reached by SkyTrain, so it's easy to spend an afternoon exploring the parks, going shopping and enjoying diversions beyond downtown.

SOUTH

Steveston

A half-hour drive (32km/20 miles) south from downtown Vancouver is Steveston at the mouth of the mighty Fraser. The river boasts the biggest salmon run in North America, and Steveston has the largest fleet of commercial fishing vessels on Canada's West Coast.

Garry Point Park

A five-minute walk west lies sandy, windswept Garry Point Park. A tiny Oriental garden, beside the broad walking path, commemorates the arrival of the first Japanese immigrants more than a century ago.

Around Moncton Street

Seafood restaurants, marine supply stores, antique shops and such shopping delights as The Country Garden Mouse (*tel: (604) 272 4752*), which stocks a selection of Canadian crafts; the Canoe Pass Gallery (*tel: (604) 272 0095*), which sells traditional Coast Indian art; and the Riverside Gallery (*tel: (604) 274 1414*), which displays work by the owner and other artists.

Steveston Museum

A collection of fishing, farming and blacksmith tools used by early Japanese settlers. Some rooms in the two-storey 1906 structure have been restored with period furniture.
3811 Moncton Street. Open: Mon–Sat 9.30am–1pm and 1.30–5pm.
Tel: (604) 271 6868.

NORTH

Across Burrard Inlet and English Bay lies Vancouver's North Shore, backed by the rugged Coast Range mountains. Rivers, creeks and canyons meander down forested slopes, cut through clusters of houses, high-rises and businesses, and terminate along park-lined shores. Scenic coastal and mountain drives, a dozen shopping areas, a few hotels, 250 restaurants, and other businesses cater to the 200,000 North Shore residents and a much greater number of visitors (*www.cnv.org*).

Cypress, Grouse and Seymour mountains, visible from almost every vantage point in Vancouver, dominate the scene. So near yet so far from downtown, these city mountains provide a recreational paradise, particularly for picnics and hiking in summer and skiing in winter. When the clouds disperse, various vantage points provide spectacular views of downtown, the Gulf Islands, the American San Juan Islands and the eternal snows of distant Mount Baker.

The Capilano River and Grouse Mountain

Grouse Mountain, 1,220m (4,003ft) high, is a mere 15 minutes by car from downtown Vancouver to the big parking lot below the Skyride. The aerial gondola then takes ten minutes to transport 100 passengers at a time up through sweeping vistas to fresh, crisp mountain air, winding trails, alpine meadows and a superb ski area.

The most developed of the city mountains, Grouse offers a variety of top options. You can hop on a helicopter (*tel: (604) 270 1484, freephone (800) 665 4354; www.helijet.com*) and fly high across Capilano Canyon and between the peaks of The Lions. Or you can enjoy

such other attractions as horse-drawn wagon rides, an adventure playground for the children, the Altitudes Bistro for relaxing, the elegant Grouse Nest Restaurant for high dining, and, in July, the hang-gliding championships, when flyers jump off the mountain and glide down towards the city. At Theatre in the Sky, watch *Born to Fly*, a journey through the scenic beauty of BC. This high-definition documentary takes you to the highest peaks of BC's mountains, across Pacific Ocean whitecaps through lush green rainforest, all from an eagle's eye view. *Every hour on the hour, 10am–9pm. Admission charge.*

On the way down, there are several stops worth making. The enormous **Cleveland Dam**, built about 40 years ago, divides the river to create Capilano Lake, which provides the water supply for the city. At the **Capilano Salmon Hatchery** (*tel: (604) 666 1790*) from July to October, returning salmon leap ladders into the hatchery, and a display shows coho, steelhead and chinook in various stages of development.

The breathtaking aerial gondola ride up to Grouse Mountain

Vancouver suburbs

The Capilano Suspension Bridge (*tel: (604) 985 7474; www.capbridge.com*), the world's oldest suspension footbridge, was originally built in 1889. The wire rope and wood structure sways and flaps 70m (230ft) above the rushing waters of the river below. The bridge stretches 137m (449ft) across the steep canyon, providing access to nature trails meandering through an old-growth forest. Splurge on fine dining at the Bridge House Restaurant, the former home of the original owner of the Capilano Bridge, or just grab a quick snack at the Canyon Café. Don't miss Treetops, the award winning attraction that lets you see the wonders of the forest from as high as 30m (100ft) above the forest floor.

For more information see www.grousemountain.com

THE LEGEND OF THE TWO SISTERS

Renamed The Lions by the British, these twin peaks rise to 1,646m (5,400ft) at the northern end of the Cypress Provincial Park wilderness. A long time ago, as a great Capilano chief prepared to celebrate the coming of age of his twin daughters, a powerful northerly tribe declared war. But the daughters persuaded their father to invite the hostile Indians to their feast, and this *potlatch* festival of peace brought friendship to the tribes. The chief decided to make his daughters immortal, and lifted them to these lofty twin peaks to stand forever as symbols of peace and friendship.

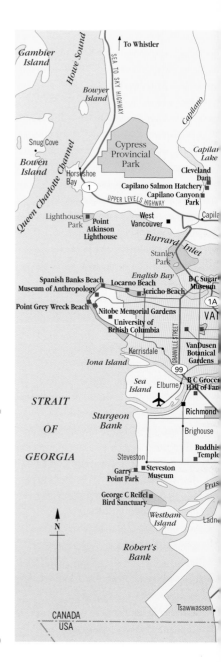

Vancouver suburbs

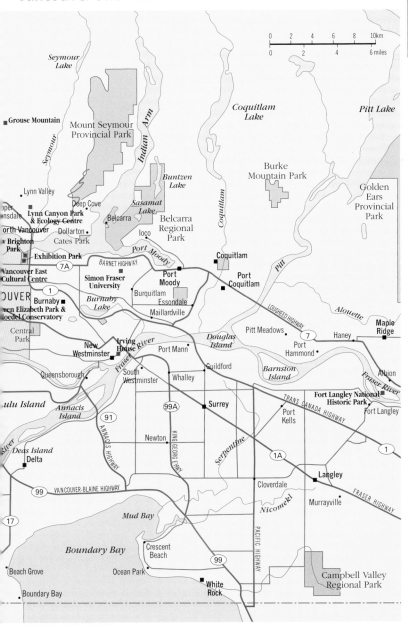

North Shore Mountains
Cypress Provincial Park

Northwest of Vancouver, overlooking Howe Sound to the west, Cypress Provincial Park provides spectacular views over the city to Mount Baker and southwest to Vancouver Island and the Gulf Islands. Excellent cross-country ski trails and good downhill runs attract Vancouverites every day and evening in winter. In summer, the main attraction is the network of hiking trails. Some, such as the Yew Lake circuit, are suitable for novices, while the Crest Trail challenges even the experts.

It takes about 20 minutes to drive to the park along the Cypress Parkway from the exit on Upper Levels Highway (Highway 1/99). The end of the road is marked by a large parking area, a cafeteria, a shop and the park administration building, where brochures illustrating the trails are available.

The forest comprises mostly evergreens, such as Douglas and

The city of Vancouver against the backdrop of Mount Seymour

amabilis fir, which thrive on this rainy coast. Deciduous trees include alders, maples and the flowering dogwood, whose neat white blossom is the provincial flower. Ferns and mosses, fed by stumps and fallen and ageing trees, flourish, and marsh marigold, skunk cabbage and salmonberries also brighten the landscape. Black bears love the berries, so be sure to give them right of way. Watchful eyes sometimes see deer feeding on the open slopes along the road. The boldest bird is the whisky jack, which lands right on picnic tables, while chickadees, nuthatches, crossbills and Steller's jays forage in the forest.
Tel: (604) 926 5612.

Mount Seymour Provincial Park

This park encompasses 3,500 hectares (8,649 acres) of wilderness, including Mount Elsay and Mount Bishop, as well as Mount Seymour (1,450m/4,757ft). It contains old-growth fir, western red and yellow cedar, and hemlock, with carpets of alpine flowers in open areas. Coyotes and deer appear sometimes, close to the highway, and hares, Douglas squirrels and martens can skirt the hiking trails. An occasional black bear or cougar has been sighted in the back country. The guided tours and displays in the Lower Seymour Conservation Reserve (*tel: (604) 990 0483*) are an excellent way to learn about local flora and fauna, rainforests and fisheries.

The winding 13km (8-mile) highway up Seymour ends at parking lot 4, near the cafeteria and chair lift. The Goldie Lake/Flower Lake Trail, a nordic ski route in winter, provides an easy and relatively flat one-hour loop, although a dozen other recommended walks are listed in the brochure available in the cafeteria. Partway down the highway, a two-hour walk along the Baden-Powell Trail leads down through thick forest and across ravines to the village of Deep Cove, on the Indian Arm, which has a sandy beach and a canoe rental shop.
Tel: (604) 986 2261.

Parks on Indian Arm

A water taxi runs across Indian Arm from **Deep Cove** to Belcarra Regional Park, which shelters Sasamat Lake, one of the warmest in the region. Cates Park, where the waters of Indian Arm and Burrard Inlet meet, is popular with scuba divers. A 15m (49ft) long war canoe, carved in an unusual chequerboard design, is displayed in the park. The nearby Malcolm Lowry Walk provides a peaceful ten-minute stroll through the leafy forest and back along the shell-strewn shore.
www.deepcovebc.com

Whistler

Named after the call of the hoary marmot, one of the first inhabitants of the area, Whistler is a top-class winter sports centre that continues to receive accolades from skiers from all over the world. And getting there is half the fun.

The Sea to Sky Highway

Appropriately called the Sea to Sky Highway, the road to Whistler fringes fiord-like Howe Sound. Here, rugged rainforest and sheer rock faces, sculpted by glaciers during the last Ice Age, ascend to meadows blanketed in summer with Indian paintbrushes and other alpine flowers, and in winter with snow.

A good picnic place along the road is **Porteau Cove**, which also offers good swimming, snorkelling, scuba diving, boating and fishing. At Britannia Beach, the **BC Mining Museum**, once the largest copper producer in the British Empire and now a National Historic Site, offers underground tours in little electric trains, and an intriguing display of old mining equipment (*tel: (604) 896 2233, freephone (800) 896 4044; www.bcmuseumofmining.org; open: mid-May–mid-Oct daily 9am–4.30pm; mid-Oct–mid-May Mon–Fri 9am–4.30pm (limited facilities); admission charge*).

The next stop should be **Shannon Falls**; *www.britishcolumbia.com/ parksandtrails/parks*. BC's third-highest waterfall thunders down a 335m (1,099ft) cliff following the trail of a slithering sea serpent, according to the local legend.

A few kilometres beyond the falls, the logging town of **Squamish** is famous as a rock-climbing centre. The Stawamus Chief, a 652m (2,139ft) high granite monolith, is second in size in the world, after the Rock of Gibraltar. Another

Shannon Falls

hour's drive past reflecting lakes and through small open valleys and forest, lies Whistler.

Whistler: the mountain playground

Whistler Village is nestled between twin mountain peaks, Whistler and Blackcomb, in the Coast Range. The village is a cluster of hotels, shops, condominiums, restaurants and cobbled walkways, constructed in a mixed West Coast and imitation European style.

A five-minute walk from the village square leads to the ski lifts which service the largest ski area and the two longest vertical drops on the continent: Blackcomb, 1,609m (5,279ft), and Whistler, 1,530m (5,020ft). The resort also has the most extensive high-speed ski-lift system in the world, with a total of 30 lifts, including three gondolas and nine quad chairs. About a quarter of the 200 downhill runs are tailored to experts, another quarter to beginners, and the rest are for intermediate skiers. Cross-country trails skirt the golf course and Lost Lake. After the warm spring sun melts the snows of winter, avid skiers head to the Horstman Glacier and share the lifts with mountain bikers, who ride down the now-gravel trails that skiers slalom in winter. Overhead, paragliders float down to the village below.

Whistler also offers an 18-hole golf course, hiking, horse riding, canoeing, river rafting, windsurfing and fishing. Musicians, magicians, clowns, comedians and jugglers entertain every

HOW TO GET THERE

You can travel to Whistler, 120km (75 miles) north of Vancouver, by Helijet (*tel: (800) 665 4354; www.helijet.com*); Maverick Coach Lines (*tel: (604) 255 1171; www.maverickcoach.com*); or drive yourself, which takes about two hours nonstop. For further information see: *www.tourismwhistler.com* or *www.whistleronline.com*

day in the streets from mid-June to September. Major festivals feature country and blues in July, classical music in August and jazz in September.

Accommodation varies, from the luxurious 343-room Château Whistler, the largest château-style property built in Canada for a century, to the rustic Riverside RV Resort and Campground. *Tel: 1 800 WHISTLER (freephone); www.tourismwhistler.com*

Panorama from Whistler mountain, looking towards Blackcomb

Animal kingdom

Vancouver is a little like The Sleeping Beauty – blessed by the good fairies at birth with great natural beauty everywhere you look. The city rests at the foot of a range of mountains and looks out to the ocean with deep inlets cutting into the land. Parks and gardens are scattered everywhere through the city, and pristine rainforest and wilderness lie just behind the last row of houses on the North Shore. Is it any wonder, then, that Vancouverites coexist harmoniously (most of the time) with critters from the forest?

In North Vancouver, signs in the parks warn of wandering bears, and local dogs stroll along wearing 'bear bells'. It's not unusual for a local matron to step outside onto the doorstep for her morning paper and see a bear walking up the driveway. Most of the time these natural encounters are uneventful,

Vancouver's many pockets of wilderness are a delight for animal lovers

An elk in the Rockies

but not too long ago a cougar wandered into Victoria and was seen prowling around the car park of the city's most famous hotel. Raccoons seem to hang out wherever there's a small stand of natural park, and in the city they can be a real nuisance on 'garbage day' along with legions of chipmunks, skunks and squirrels. The city's most famous park – the 440-hectare (1,087-acre) Stanley Park – is a thickly wooded tract of cedar, hemlock and fir and has its own battalion of raccoons that will shamelessly beg for French fries or popcorn. Park officials discourage visitors from feeding these beggars

since they can bite. Even more dangerous are the minefields of poop left by the park's beautiful but messy Canada geese.

In the Fraser Valley to the east of the city and beyond, you can see fields of ordinary farm animals but also more exotic species such as llamas and alpacas that are being raised as pets, for their wool or as guide animals. On the Gulf Islands and on Vancouver Island deer can be so plentiful they are considered pests, and on a train ride further into the province there's a good chance of catching a herd of bighorn sheep grazing by the tracks.

Walk: Bowen Island

Bowen Island is located northwest of Vancouver – a 20-minute ferry ride from Horseshoe Bay to Snug Cove. It is a wonderful day trip from Vancouver. This lush, green, bowl-shaped isle, capped by 760m (2,493ft) Mount Gardner, has long been a holiday hideaway for Vancouverites.

Allow a day for the trip.

By car the drive takes half an hour; head northwest along Georgia Street, across the Lions Gate Bridge and follow the ferry signs west along the Upper Levels Highway. There is usually ample parking in Horseshoe Bay, except on holiday weekends. A car is not necessary on the island; board the ferry as a foot passenger.

As the ferry rounds the point from Horseshoe Bay into Queen Charlotte Sound, the Lions and the Howe Sound Crest mountains appear dramatically outlined against the sky. South across the water lies little Passage Island, Point Atkinson lighthouse and, across English Bay, Point Grey.

From the ferry dock in Snug Cove, it is a three-minute walk along Government Road to the commercial centre of the island.

This main square has a couple of pubs, restaurants with flower-decked patios, craft shops, bakeries, and the restored Union Steamship Company Store, now the local library. It's just a short walk to the Visitor Information Centre at 432 Cardena Road.

Detour right before the store where a short, tree-lined road leads to a freshwater lagoon on one side and the calm waters of Deep Bay on the other. Opposite Cardena Drive, a green sign indicates a leafy trail that marks the entrance to Crippen Regional Park and the Killarney Lake Trail.

It is a 6km (4-mile) round trip. The trail is wide and fairly flat, except for a few steep sections. For a leisurely stroll, allow about two hours.

A few minutes along the trail, the sound of plunging Terminal Creek announces two fish ladders zigzagging up the rocky hillside beside the creek. During October and November, salmon that went to sea after being raised in a nearby hatchery return after two or three years to leap the ladders upstream and spawn in the waters they came from.

The trail, flanked by leafy screens of trees, emerges on to Miller Road. About 100m (328ft) to the right, the trail continues on the other side. A second-growth forest of red cedars, hemlocks and maples towers over a tangled undergrowth where huge stumps still remain as reminders of earlier logging.

The trail crosses Magee Road to the Killarney Lake Loop Trail, where bikes and horses are not allowed. The main trail heads north around the lake to a gravel beach with picnic tables, toilets and a small swimming area.

The trail climbs slightly to join a broad boardwalk over a marsh where Labrador tea, bog laurel, sweet gale bushes and the carnivorous sundew plant thrive. In early summer brilliant yellow skunk cabbage, which smells like it sounds, glows in the underbrush. Blue herons hunch patiently in the shallow water, waiting for dinner to swim by. The trail meanders on, with frequent views of the lake and the forested foothills around Mount Gardner.

Follow the signs back to Snug Cove to catch the ferry back to the mainland. From downtown Vancouver, take the Blue Bus (tel: (604) 985 7777) on Georgia St, which runs every half-hour to Horseshoe Bay. Allow an hour for the bus trip. Bus No 250 follows scenic Marine Drive through West Vancouver and Bus No 257 follows the highway. Most visitors arrive aboard BC Ferries Howe Sound Queen (tel: 1-888-BCFERRY; www.bcferries.com). For more information, tel: (250) 947 9024; fax: (250) 947 0633; www.bowenisland.org

WEST

Mention West Vancouver and most Canadians conjure up images of sprawling, million-dollar waterfront mansions backed by park-like gardens, and patio drives filled with Mercedes and Jaguars. It is true that the municipality's 40,000 residents do boast the highest per capita income in Canada. The most well-known luxurious residential area is called The British Properties. But many small clapboard cottages, built as summer homes long before the Guinness family built the Lions Gate Bridge in 1938, still survive here untouched by developers, and are valued at prices far lower than the current value of the land they occupy.

West Vancouver is not the Wild West. About 20 per cent of West Vaners are pensioned senior citizens. There is little crime and no industry. The suburb snakes for 20km (12 miles) along the north shore of English Bay from the Lions Gate Bridge to Horseshoe Bay, and climbs about 5km (3 miles) up the slope towards Cypress Mountain. West Vancouver has over 100 parks and over 100km (62 miles) of paths and trails connecting the community. Once people have lived here, they say they would not want to live anywhere else in Canada, even though commuters encounter frequent waits in summer to cross the bridge to the big city.

For browsing or buying, West Vancouver has the Park Royal Shopping Centre and a good range of little stores in Ambleside village and in the one block between 24th and 25th Street called Dundarave. Visitors can also enjoy fishing, golfing, tennis at free public courts, lawn bowling, swimming and exercise at several fitness circuits.

Ferry building

Built in 1913, this heritage building, which is now a waterfront gallery, was once a meeting place for residents arriving from and leaving for downtown Vancouver. The adjacent waterfront park, known as Ambleside Landing, offers a view of Prospect Point in Stanley Park, and features a fountain sculpture and a fishing pier complete with cleaning table.
1414 Argyle Ave. Tel: (604) 925 7290.
Open: Tue–Sun 11am–5pm;
Fri 10am–8pm.

Gertrude Lawson House

Home to the West Vancouver Museum and Archives, this old ballast-stone house was built in 1940 by Gertrude Lawson, daughter of the Father of West Vancouver, businessman John Lawson. It is now a museum relating the history of the area. The unusual stone façade of the house echoes the architectural character of the grand homes of Scotland which Ms Lawson greatly admired. The stones are themselves believed to have come from New Zealand as ballast on timber trading ships.
680 17th St. Tel: (604) 925 7295.
Open: Tue–Sat 11am–5pm.
Admission charge.

Parks and walkways

Gardens, parks and walkways are everywhere. Ambleside Park is a great place to see residents walking their dogs. The spectacular 2km (1¹/₄-mile) paved Seawalk has a fenced-off trail for four-footed friends. The best beach is the little one near Dundarave Pier, between 14th and Bellevue, where concession stands sell summer snacks for beachcombers. This is also a popular place for summer crabbing and fishing. Westward, a pebbled shore strewn with driftwood, is a great place for beachcombing. Caulfield Park, which has a forested path along the waterfront, is famous for its flush toilets!

Lighthouse Park, a treasure hidden away further west along Marine Drive, has a labyrinth of trails through an enchanted forest of giant Douglas firs, pines, hemlocks and arbutus trees, recognisable by their smooth, peeling rust-red bark. The Point Atkinson Lighthouse, built in 1912, is one of the few working lighthouses left in the province. The promontory just west of the lighthouse offers views of freighters anchored in English Bay, Point Grey and the mountains of Vancouver Island.

EAST
Lower Mainland
Fort Langley

An hour's drive east from Vancouver's chrome and glass high-rises is the historic little village of Fort Langley, the site of the original fort and

Lions Gate Bridge spans Burrard Inlet, linking downtown with the North Shore

Vancouver suburbs

THE HUDSON'S BAY COMPANY

This company of English adventurers formed in 1670, during the reign of King Charles II, to trade in North America throughout the lands that drained into Hudson's Bay.

The commercial empire that grew out of it began with a few shiploads of British goods being traded for furs, and at one time it was the largest landowner in the world. After numerous dramatic struggles, a merger with the North West Company took place in 1821.

When Canada became a country, the Hudson's Bay Company gave up its trade monopoly, but retained its forts and trading posts. Eventually, a chain of Hudson's Bay department stores was built in western Canada and still exists today. Small Bay stores remain as the commercial centres of several remote settlements scattered throughout the Canadian Arctic.

fur-trading post where BC began. It was here that BC was declared a Crown Colony in 1858.

Fort Langley village has, so far, escaped the contrived charm which often accompanies historical reconstructions. This can be attributed to the fact that most of its quaint clapboard churches, antique shops and false-fronted buildings are original.

Near the fort, the **BC Farm Museum** (*9131 King St. Tel: (604) 888 2273*) houses a comprehensive collection of steam tractors, stump pullers, ploughs, reapers, harvesters, buckboards, a working sawmill and a vintage Tiger Moth plane – the first crop duster in the province.

The **Langley Centennial Museum**, next door, displays numerous Coast Salish Indian artefacts and a selection of 19th-century pioneer crafts and furnishings.

Fort Langley National Historic Site

First built in 1839, Fort Langley was once the Hudson's Bay Company's most important provisioning post in the Pacific Northwest, and has been reconstructed to recreate the past. Within the palisaded high wooden walls, the Big House, the bastion, a cooperage and carpentry shop, and a blacksmith's forge have been rebuilt. The storehouse, the only original structure on site, is stacked with furs, clothing, trapping equipment, trading goods and other supplies used by fur traders, gold miners, Indians and other 19th-century residents.

Interpreters in period costumes demonstrate pioneer life at the fort. Some are blacksmiths fashioning tools; some are coopers building barrels, which were once used to ship salmon and other foodstuffs from the fort; and some bake salmon and bannock in open outdoor ovens for sampling.

Other interpreters present talks and organise games to help children enjoy learning local history. Coast Salish Natives from neighbouring MacMillan Island often work at the fort constructing canoes, carving paddles and making jewellery.

The Big House replicates the original building which was pulled down in 1886. The refurbished parlour suggests

A costumed interpreter at Fort Langley

the relative luxury the chief trader and his family enjoyed, and an intriguing diary displayed in the big hall describes early life at the fort.

Brigade Days, held in early August, re-enact the fur brigades arriving to trade at Fort Langley after weeks of canoeing south through networks of rivers. Douglas Day, in mid-November, is another colourful ceremony, which commemorates the inauguration of BC.

The Friends of the Fort gift shop stocks a variety of souvenirs, including reproductions of old trading goods. *23433 Mavis St. Tel: (604) 513 4777. www.pc.gc.ca/fortlangley. Open: daily Sept–June 10am–5pm; July–Aug daily 9am–8pm. Admission charge.*

The Native riverboat trip

A pleasant way to visit Fort Langley is aboard *The Native*, a working replica of a late 19th-century paddlewheeler. This 100-passenger vessel follows the Fraser River upstream from New Westminster to Fort Langley. The four-hour journey traces the route taken by fortune hunters, fur traders, miners, merchants, millionaires and stagecoach robbers during the 19th century. Native Indians also canoed the route while fishing, hunting and trapping. The excursion is narrated, with extracts by early explorers. The company runs both lunch and dinner cruises. *139–810 Quayside, New Westminster. Tel: (604) 525 4465; www.vancouverpaddlewheeler.com*

Harrison Hot Springs

These hot springs were discovered rather dramatically during the 1850s when a clumsy prospector was tipped out of his canoe into Harrison Lake. He was dumbfounded to find the water not frigid, but warm. Word spread and, for later prospectors on the gold rush trail, Harrison Hot Springs became a popular stopover site.

Although Harrison Hot Springs Hotel is today in the luxury category, anyone can enjoy such specialities as lobster mousse or poached salmon in the restaurant and look out at the lake. There is also plenty of less expensive hotel, motel and campground accommodation. Other restaurants line the lakeshore.

Shoppers and browsers can enjoy a range of shops offering everything from video rentals, camping supplies and Canadiana to the Christmas decorations sold year-round in the cosy Holly Tree Place.

Soothing spring waters

Two springs percolate from the base of nearby mountains. A sulphur spring, about two-thirds sodium sulphate and sodium chloride, flows out at 68°C (154°F). A potash spring, with potassium chloride and sodium sulphate making up more than half its mineral content, enters the lake at 71°C (160°F). Both spring waters also contain lime and magnesium sulphates, sulphurated hydrogen and bicarbonates of lime and iron. To see the springs

bubbling up from their source, walk westward along the dyke beside the lake and past the hotel.

A pipe system carries the mineral waters to the hotel and public pools, for which there is an admission charge. The water is stored in huge tanks and cooled to 38°C (100°F), the perfect temperature for a soothing soak. Massages are available.

Outdoor activities and sport

The town of Harrison Hot Springs offers a great variety of activities for lovers of the outdoors. Boaters enjoy exploring the lake, which stretches 60km (37 miles) north, but watch for strong thermal winds which may rise rapidly shortly after noon on a summer day. The morning calm is great for waterskiing, and the afternoon winds are great for windsurfing. Other outdoor options include golf, tennis, cycling, croquet, horseshoes and shuffleboard.

Numerous walking and hiking trails provide easy access to the forests and mountains. The easiest one, about 2km (1^1/$_4$ miles) long, follows the lake from the Harrison Hot Springs Hotel to the boat launch and around the lagoon, while the Campbell Lake Trail, which requires more than four hours, rises a challenging 600m (1,969ft) to a beautiful mountain lake.

The Sasquatch Daze in May, Days of Wine & Roses in June and the Sandsculpture Competition in early September attract many visitors to

Harrison Hot Springs every year. The record for the world's tallest sandcastle was set here in 1990.

There is a parade of gaily lit boats on the lake during the evening of 1 July, Canada Day. The week-long Festival of the Arts, later in July, features a spectrum of artistic expression in music, dance, theatre and visual art, and artefacts. A special day set aside for children includes storytellers, face-painting, workshops and other activities, and a writers' evening offers readings with Canadian authors.
Tel: (604) 796 3664; www.harrison.ca, www.harrisonfestival.com

Minter Gardens

Tucked away a few metres west off Yale Road, just after the turn-off north from Highway 1 to Harrison Hot Springs, are the Minter Gardens. Pathways wind through 11 hectares (27 acres) of sights, sounds, fragrances, textures and tastes. In springtime, tulips, daffodils, hyacinths, primulas, rhododendrons and azaleas blaze with colour. Summer brings a prize display of annuals, and autumn presents a shower of falling leaves in green, gold and red, backdropped by 2,134m (7,001ft) Mount Cheam. Other highlights include the Rose Garden, which blossoms most of the year; topiaries of southern belles and northern deer; a rare collection of Penjing rock bonsai; and a fragrance trail for the blind.
Tel: (604) 794 7191, freephone 1 888 646 8377; www.mintergardens.com. Open: Apr–Oct daily 9am–sunset. Admission charge. Free parking.

Minter Gardens are a riot of flowers in the summer

Peace Arch Park

Canada, the second-largest country in area on earth (after Russia), and the USA have the longest undefended international border in the world, stretching 6,500km (4,040 miles) from the Atlantic Ocean to the Pacific. Shared by both countries, the Peace Arch Park at the southern end of Highway 99 in BC may be one of the most beautiful border crossings anywhere.

A monument to peace

The idea of a peace arch was conceived by the late Samuel Hill of Seattle to commemorate a permanent peace between Canada and the USA. While president of the Pacific Highway Association, Hill, a road builder and Quaker, proposed that an arch be constructed at the centenary of the signing of the Treaty of Ghent in 1814. The treaty marked the end of the War of 1812 between Great Britain and the USA, resolving the ongoing conflict between the two powers at that time. The Peace Arch, the first such structure in the world, became a reality in 1921 and marked the 300th anniversary of the sailing of the Pilgrim Fathers to America.

Built of concrete reinforced with steel, in Greek Doric style, the arch was designed to vibrate but not crack in case of an earthquake. The gleaming white open portal, which stands about 30m (98ft) high, flies the Canadian and American flags side by side. Across the top on the American side is the inscription 'Children of a Common Mother'. The Canadian side reads 'Brethren Dwelling Together in Unity'.

Two iron gates span the opening that leads from one country to the other. Here children and adults from both countries like to stand, with one foot planted on Canadian soil, the other in the USA. In a celebration held in early June every year, children from both countries meet here and file through the portal and exchange flags. Over the west gate is written '1814 – Open for One Hundred Years – 1914' and over the east 'May These Gates Never Be Closed'.

Originally incorporated into the Canadian side was a beam from the SS *Beaver*, which in 1836 became the first steamship to enter the Pacific Ocean. A beam of wood from the hull of *The Mayflower*, the ship that carried the Pilgrim Fathers to America in 1621, was embedded into the American side. These relics have since been removed and stored elsewhere for future generations.

A garden of harmony

During the 1920s, some peace lovers banded together to raise funds to purchase land surrounding the Peace Arch for a park. BC schoolchildren responded, some with only a penny, others with as much as 10 cents. More than $2,000 was raised, quite a lot in those days. The money was applied to the purchase of a portion of the property. Other funds were eventually found and 9 hectares (22 acres) were set aside as the **Peace Arch Park**. The 7 hectares (17 acres) that make up the Washington State Peace Arch Park were eventually acquired in a similar fashion.

Today, the Peace Arch serves as a symbol to remind all passing by that neighbours can live together in peace. The portal is the centrepiece for the surrounding broad green lawns, flower gardens, rockeries, playgrounds, picnic areas, shelters and kitchens that have been built on both sides over the years. The Canadian side features a wooden gazebo, a lily pond and a rectangle of red and white blossoms representing the Canadian flag. To the west, a cliff overlooks the old Burlington Northern Railway line and the waters of Semiahmoo Bay, which wash the shores of both countries.

The symbolic open portal that bridges the national boundaries of Canada and the USA

Flowers in season

When most people think of BC they envisage a land blanketed in greenery. The Lower Mainland region does tend to remain eternally leafy, thanks to the temperate climate and abundant rains.

It is usually March when the first crocuses, daffodils, tulips and hyacinths burst forth. Bold umbrellas of pink unfold on Japanese cherry trees along city streets; magnolias and camellias bloom in delicate whites and pinks, and the japonica bushes open bright clusters of flowers resembling apple blossoms. Forsythia shrubs produce golden streamers and wisterias wind long tassels of purple along building walls. Yellow skunk cabbages, which smell like they sound, brighten dank forest areas in Stanley Park.

In June, azaleas and rhododendrons, dressed in brilliant hues of pink, salmon, coral and crimson, announce the advent of summer. Roses bloom in town and country gardens, and wild lupins brighten the roadsides. Dahlias, delphiniums, phlox, asters and poppies share the summer sun with sweet peas, gladioli, freesias, zinnias, marigolds and nasturtiums, while fuchsias and busy Lizzies thrive in the shade. Moss-packed hanging baskets sport trailing lobelias and verbenas, mingled with petunias and pelargoniums.

The late summer display includes snapdragons, primroses, wallflowers and Canterbury bells. As the golden autumn leaves fall from the trees,

Summer months bring a riot of Nicotiana

Whatever the season may be, BC's gardens and parks are always in full bloom

irises, cat-tails (or reedmace) and marsh marigolds begin to flower near ponds and lakes.

Even the grey winter is brightened by flowering plants. Clumps of white and pink heather border lawns, while window boxes appear colourful with winter pansies and curly kale. Some roses, along with the pretty blossoms of the winter-flowering plum and the yellow trumpets of winter jasmine, smile right through a short snowfall. Holly outside and poinsettias inside follow the Christmas tradition of red and green. Red-osier dogwoods, the bright yellow twigs of Siberian dogwood and clusters of bright pink berries on the spindleberry bush also liven the winter landscape.

Vancouver's islands

Almost 200 islands of all shapes and sizes lie between the Lower Mainland and Vancouver Island (see map pp104–5). Some of these Gulf Islands offer superb natural scenery, outdoor activities, accommodation and food. Although locals love the quiet winters, the islands are much livelier in summer when visitors come from all over the world for the spectacular water views, the balmy climate, the abundant sunshine and the gentle lifestyle.

For more information visit www.vancouverisland.travel

GULF ISLANDS

The six major inhabited Gulf Islands are Saltspring, North and South Pender, Galiano, Mayne and Saturna. Saltspring is the most developed and the most densely populated. But Mayne, which is not the principal island, is preferred by many visitors. About 8km by 5km (5 miles by 3 miles) in area, Mayne Island has only 900 year-round residents. They are mostly artists and artisans, a few business people, and others who have retired to enjoy a leisurely island lifestyle.

Like the other Gulf Islands, Mayne is mainly bays and beaches, and gentle wooded hills of arbutus, Douglas fir, alder, cedar and brilliant bursts of broom, although early settlers did clear some land for farming.

Popular activities include swimming, scuba diving, fishing, canoeing, kayaking, clam digging, beachcombing, hiking and cycling.

The Gulf Islands are popular precisely because there is little organised activity. On Mayne, Blue Vista (*tel: (250) 539 2463, freephone (877) 535 2424*) does rent out kayaks and bikes, and leads interpretive kayak tours. Mayne Island Kayak, Canoe & Bike Rentals (*tel: (250) 539 5599*) also rents and has guided tours and instruction. Most Mayne roads are hilly, but asphalted. Get natural eats at Happy Tides or find something locally grown at the seasonal farmer's market.

Most of the Gulf Islands are accessible year-round via BC Ferries (*tel: 1 888 BCFERRY or (250) 386 343; www.bcferries.com*) and Harbour Air (*freephone (800) 665 0212; www.harbour-air.com*). Ferries to the islands leave Tsawwassen on the mainland 30km (19 miles) south of Vancouver. Many boaters prefer to visit in their own craft, finding shelter and moorage at numerous bays throughout the islands.

Mayne Island

While the wilderness is wonderful, Mayne Island offers a wholesome portion of history as well. Native tribes inhabited Helen Point 5,000 years ago. Evidence remains in the middens and white beaches formed from eroded clam, abalone and oyster shells. In the late 1850s, rowdy miners stopped here en route from Victoria to the goldfields of Barkerville; some returned to enjoy the relatively mild winters. At the turn of the last century, British gentry liked to spend their summers on Mayne.

The lighthouse at Georgina Point, built in 1855, still guides vessels into the eastern entrance to Active Pass. The lighthouse is open to visitors every day from 1pm to 3pm (no admission charge).

For more information on the Gulf Islands, contact Tourism Association of Vancouver Island, *203–335 Wesley St, Nanaimo. Tel: (250) 754 3500.* Also see *www.gulfislands.net*

The best-loved country church on Mayne Island is St Mary Magdalene's, built in 1898 on a hill overlooking Active Pass. The 180kg (397lb) sandstone font was carried by rowing boat from Saturna Island in 1900.

The Mayne Island Gaol is open in summer (no admission charge). Built in 1896, it is now a museum housing memorabilia from the 19th century, including remnants from the sailing barque *Zephyr* which hit the Georgina shoals and sank in 1872. Check out *www.mayneislandchamber.ca*

Vancouver's islands

The Village Bay ferry dock on Mayne Island

Galiano Island

Coon Bay, Bluff Park, Mt Sutil and Mt Galiano have fine views. Montague Provincial Park offers wildlife (*for more information see www.galianoisland.com*).

Pender Islands

Famous for beaches and coves, and the Driftwood Centre and craft shops at Port Washington, as well as wildlife. *Events: Salmon BBQ and Fish Derby (July); Art Show, Fall Fair (Aug).* www.penderisland.info

Saltspring Island

Look out for art and craft galleries, village shops and the Saturday-morning market at Ganges. Views at Mt Maxwell and Ruckle Provincial Park are superb. *Events: Round the Island Race (May); Sea Capers (June); Art/Craft Exhibition (June–Sept); Fall Fair (Sept).* www.saltspringisland.org

Saturna Island

East Point Lighthouse, Saturna pub and store, and Winter Cove Marine Park are all worth a visit. Wildlife, including ravens and wild goats, can be seen. *Events: Lamb Barbecue (July).* www.saturnatourism.com

HAIDA GWAII (QUEEN CHARLOTTE ISLANDS)

The Charlottes, named Haida Gwaii by the native Haida people, comprise two main islands, **Graham** and **Moresby**, and 150 little ones, together covering an

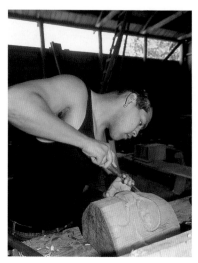
Haida craftsman at work

area of 9,000sq km (3,475sq miles). They lie north of Vancouver Island and about 120km (75 miles) west of Prince Rupert (*see map on pp22–3*). Frequently hidden under a grey blanket of cloud and fog, Haida Gwaii is surrounded by treacherous seas and rocks. The Cape St James weather station, hugging the southern tip of the southernmost island, is the windiest one in Canada. But it is also the warmest, thanks to soothing Kuroshio currents crossing the Pacific Ocean from Japan.

Much of empty Moresby Island is parkland, a result of efforts by Haida and other environmentalists. Although fishermen by tradition, the 2,000 Haida who live here today are celebrated for beautifully carved wooden masks, canoes, totem poles, and smaller items shaped in argillite, an ebony slate mudstone. A few hundred years ago, about 8,000 Haida lived here, famed in the region as fierce warriors. But they were decimated by Caucasian diseases, probably beginning in 1774, when the first European, Juan José Pérez, sailed round the northern coast.

Grey, weathered totem poles still stand at several abandoned villages throughout these rugged isles. The most accessible is Yan, in the north of Graham Island. A visiting permit can be purchased from the local chief, who can arrange boats and guides. The Haida, who claim 10,000 years of experience, also organise tours to the South Moresby National Park and Ninstints (**Anthony Island**), site of the largest cluster of original standing totem poles in the world.

Although about 6,000 people in all now live in Haida Gwaii, there are no banks or shopping malls. The isolation and the mists have, over the years, attracted many interesting characters, some who came to the islands because they were different, and others who became different because they came to the islands.

The moss-draped forests of the Galapagos North, as Haida Gwaii is sometimes called, provide a dreamy silence for the shy black-tailed deer, Roosevelt elk and black bear that live in them. On the eastern shores, where the murmuring sea washes broad crescents of pebbles and sand, loons call soulfully over the waters and bald eagles squeal overhead from shadowing stands of ancient cedar and Sitka spruce. Whales,

sea lions, porpoises and puffins live offshore. Anglers usually go home with catches of rock and ling cod, salmon, halibut, trout and red snapper. Fishing remains a strong industry, but logging is fast disappearing.

For more information see www.haidagwaiitourism.ca

Delkatla Wildlife Sanctuary

This park is of special interest to birdwatchers because of the more than 100 native and migrating species of birds that have been spotted here, including auklets, petrels, puffins and sandhill cranes.

On a salt marsh near Masset, Graham Island. Tel: (250) 626 5015; www.birdsanctuary.org. Open: daily.

Haida Heritage Centre

The Haida Heritage Centre at Qay'llnagaay on Graham Island includes a series of traditional Haida cedar longhouses. The modern replicas

---

HOW TO GET THERE

Air Canada (*tel: 1 888 247 2262; www.aircanada.com*) jets twice daily from Vancouver to Sandspit on northeast Moresby Island. You can also fly from Prince Rupert with Harbour Air to Sandspit on Moresby Island. Car rental is expensive and getting around the islands is difficult. BC Ferries (*tel: 1 888 BCFERRY or (604) 386 3431*) make the six-hour run from Prince Rupert to Skidegate every day in summer, and three times weekly in winter. A 20-minute ferry runs every hour or two between Moresby Island and Graham Island, where most of the relatively small choice of motels and hotels are located.

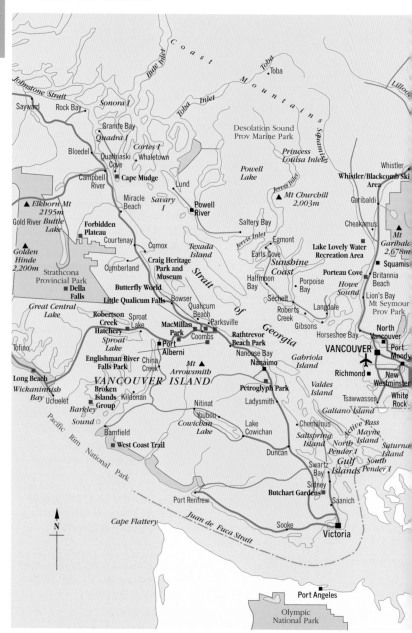

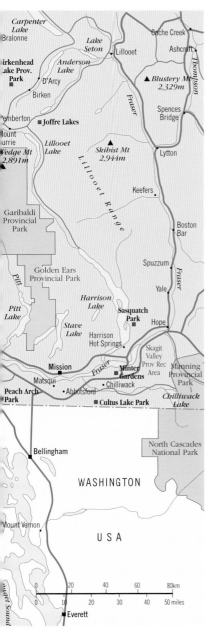

serve as a home for Haida culture and a place to learn and share Haida life. This new complex includes monumental totem poles, modern work and historical Haida art, and photo archives. Events include Skidegate Days in July, and seafood dinners followed by traditional Haida dances.

Tel: (250) 559 7885; www.haidaheritagecentre.com. Open: summer Mon–Fri 10am–6pm, Sat, Sun & holidays 10am–5pm; winter call for hours. Admission charge.

Naikoon Provincial Park

Naikoon (means 'rose point' in Haida) Park, set in 72,640 hectares (179,491 acres), offers 100km (62 miles) of beaches. It contains many hiking trails, including one to Tow Hill, which overlooks an agate beach and an unusual lava formation. Sitka deer and the rare Peale's peregrine falcon can be spotted here.

On the east coast between Tlell and Masset, Graham Island. Tel: (250) 557 4390. Open: daily. Parking fee.

QUADRA ISLAND

Quadra Island lies off Vancouver Island's northeast coast, just a ten-minute ferry ride across Discovery Passage from the salmon-fishing centre of Campbell River.

In addition to native Indian culture and regional cuisine, the island offers many options for outdoor recreation, including kayaking, canoeing, scuba diving, whale watching and fishing.

HOW TO GET THERE

There are regular scheduled flights from Vancouver Airport to Campbell River, and a daily floatplane service from Coal Harbour to Campbell River.

Landlubbers can enjoy beachcombing at Rebecca Spit, hiking the trails or climbing up Chinese Mountain for the spectacular view, and mountain biking.

For history buffs, there are interesting ruins to explore at the Lucky Jim Mine, and ancient Indian petroglyphs or stone drawings at Francisco Point, We-wai-kai Beach and Cape Mudge.

Kwagiulth Museum and Cultural Centre

The Potlatch Collection at the Kwagiulth Museum and Cultural Centre at Cape Mudge Village features sacred ceremonial objects such as masks, headdresses, coppers and other regalia used in Kwagiulth winter ceremonies. There's a vintage photograph collection, gift shop and, on a nearby beach, over 50 ancient petroglyphs.

37 Weway Rd, Cape Mudge. Tel: (250) 285 3733. Open: Mon–Sat 10am– 4.30pm, Sun noon–4.30pm. Closed: Sun Oct–May. Admission charge.

VANCOUVER ISLAND

Islands conjure up all kinds of images, and Vancouver Island is no exception. Stretching 450km (280 miles) along Canada's Pacific coast, this huge island

brings to mind images of mossy, dense and dark rainforests of fir, cedar and hemlock; barren, wind- and surf-swept Pacific beaches; Edwardian lampposts draped with baskets of trailing flowers; and elegant Victorian afternoon teas.

Victoria

BC is no longer predominantly British, as more and more people from different cultures and countries around the world continue to move here to live. But Victoria, the provincial capital, which began as a Hudson's Bay trading post in 1843, still retains some elements of British life – traditional afternoon tea, and a sense of propriety and order. Victorians, like many island people, tend to be more relaxed and forgiving. Perhaps this is because the

Victoria

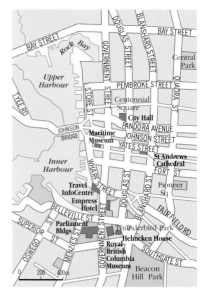

The Butchart Gardens, north of Victoria, are a showcase of floral displays

sun shines more than in Vancouver, a mere 100km (62 miles) north.

With its historic buildings, colourful old Chinatown, museums and lovely parks and gardens, Victoria offers visitors much to see and do. But for a different day, call Victoria Carriage Tours (*tel: (250) 383 2207, freephone (877) 663 2207; www.victoriacarriage.com*), and ride around the city in a classic vintage carriage drawn by a single white horse.

Alternatively, take a harbour cruise, go fishing, or splash away a summer day at the All Fun Waterslides on Millstream Road, a 15-minute drive from the city centre (*tel: (250) 474 3184; open: only in the summer*).

Butchart Gardens

Possibly the most spectacular floral display on the continent today, these gardens began as an abandoned limestone quarry in 1904. Meandering paved pathways lead through 20 hectares (49 acres) of exquisite arrangements of more than 5,000 varieties of trees, shrubs and flowers. There is a sunken

garden, rose garden, Japanese garden, Italian garden, star pond, concert lawn, fireworks basin, show greenhouse, seed store, two restaurants and a coffee bar.

In summer, additional entertainment includes musical reviews, puppet shows, night illuminations and fireworks, while in winter, after the kaleidoscope of colourful blossoms has faded, ribbons of lights brighten the grey days. Wheelchairs, cameras, baby pushcarts and umbrellas are available for hire.
800 Benvenuto Ave, about 21km (13 miles) north of Victoria via Highway 17 and Keating Cross Rd. Tel: freephone 1 866 652 4422; www.butchartgardens.com. Open: daily 9am. Closing times vary – call or visit website.

Helmcken House

The oldest house in BC open to the public was built in 1842. It provides a glimpse into the life of a pioneer physician 150 years ago. The house has become part of the Royal BC Museum.
251 Superior St. For more information, contact the Royal BC Museum, tel: (250) 356 7226, freephone (888) 447 7977. Open: June–Sept noon–4pm.

Parliament Buildings

Hourly guided tours show off this stately greystone structure and its

For information on other attractions and activities, visit the *Travel InfoCentre* which is situated at *812 Wharf St. Tel: (250) 382 2127; www.tourismvictoria.com*

intricate stained-glass windows, Italian marble panels, mosaic tile floors and painted murals illustrating the farming, fishing, mining and logging past of the province.

On the Inner Harbour. Tel: (250) 387 3046; www.parl-bldgs.gov.bc.ca. Open: Mon–Fri 9am–5pm; summer weekends (May–Sept) 9am–5pm.

Royal BC Museum

The Royal BC Museum rates in many people's eyes as the finest museum in Canada, with displays of BC history which include a woolly mammoth, cobblestone streets bordered by Victorian storefronts, a working gold-rush waterwheel, a replica of Captain George Vancouver's ship *Discovery* and the magical masks and totem poles of the First Nations.

675 Belleville St. Tel: (250) 356 7226; www.royalbcmuseum.bc.ca. Open: daily 9am–5pm. Admission charge.

Thunderbird Park

This downtown park has an outdoor display of replicas of old totem poles and original contemporary poles, and carvings by coastal Indian artists.

Beside Helmcken House.

North to Nanaimo
'The Little Town That Did'

An hour's drive north from Victoria on the Malahat Highway (Highway 1) is the little coastal town of **Chemainus**. In the early 1980s, when the century-old sawmill closed and the town lay dying, a few artists began drawing larger-than-life murals on the exterior walls of buildings. Today, the town boasts Canada's largest outdoor art gallery, with 36 murals depicting the history of the Chemainus Valley. Subjects range from a 19th-century brigantine to Hong Hing's grocery store and portraits of First Nations people.

The town also has antique shops, art galleries, boutiques selling local crafts and souvenirs, and ice-cream parlours. A friendly place for lunch is The Willow Street Café, lodged in a 100-year-old heritage building. Try some quesadillas or daily special lunches on the spacious outdoor patio (*tel: (250) 246 2434. Open: daily 9am–5pm*). The annual Festival of Murals in July and August is a lively affair; you can see painters and sculptors at work, puppeteers, dramatists, street dances and parades.

Wayside diversions

Three kilometres south of Nanaimo, right beside the road from Victoria, is tiny **Petroglyph Park**. If you blink, you might miss it. A short stroll through the woods leads to a series of ancient Indian rock carvings depicting people, birds, bottomfish and the mythical seawolf.

'The Harbour City'

Nanaimo is best known as the 'Bathtub Capital of the World', referring to the annual mid-July festival when dozens of

SNORKELLING WITH SALMON

If any life form can be called totemic for British Columbia, it's the salmon. For centuries, the many species (coho, steelhead, chum, Chinook, pink and sockeye) formed the basis of the First Nations diet and inspired their art. Today its popularity continues not only as a delicious food and for sports fishing, but also as one of BC's newest adventures – snorkelling with salmon. A company called Paradise Found in Campbell River provides wet suits, guides and all the necessary snorkelling gear. Peeking at the fish in deep eddies, running the rapids or simply floating along with schools of salmon all around is a true adrenaline high.
Paradise Found Adventure Tours. *Tel: (250) 923 0848; info@paradisefound.bc.ca; www.paradisefound.bc.ca*

tubbers challenge the often choppy waters to race 54km (34 miles) across Georgia Strait to Kitsilano Beach in Vancouver (*www. bathtub.island.net*). Also called 'The Harbour City', Nanaimo is a key link in the BC Ferries chain, with frequent regular sailings to and from Tsawwassen and Horseshoe Bay on the Lower Mainland.

A walking tour of the old town should include the Nanaimo District Museum, 100 Cameron Street (*tel: (250) 753 1821*), which has exhibits explaining such events as the arrival of the Spanish, and discovery of coal, as well as artefacts of Vancouver Island's native peoples. The highlight of the area is The Bastion, on Front Street, built by the Hudson's Bay Company in 1853 to protect settlers from attack. Today it serves as a landmark and is guarded by two of its original cannons.

Nanaimo is also famous for its chocolate bars called Nanaimo Bars. The bars comprise butter, icing sugar, a mixture of graham crackers and coconut, wrapped in rich layers of chocolate.

Although several typical restaurants such as The Blue Ginger (*5769 Turner Rd; tel: (250) 751 8238*) and the Lighthouse Bistro (*50 Anchor Way; tel: (250) 754 3212*) specialise in local seafood, the Mexican food at Gina's (*tel: (250) 753 5411*) is more fun. Perched on a clifftop across from the law courts, this cosy little restaurant is friendly, prices are reasonable, the clientele interesting and the sunset views superb. Nanaimo claims more retail space per head than any other place in North America, so shoppers can have lots of fun.

A mural in Chemainus

BC's birdlife

The rich and diverse opportunities for birdwatching in BC are a delight for expert ornithologists and amateur birdwatchers alike

Both ornithologists and amateur naturalists love BC birdwatching, one of the fastest-growing recreational activities in the province. BC is home to some 400 species of birds, representing more than 80 per cent of all the species found in Canada. Birds are not only much less elusive than other wild creatures in BC, but also offer cheery songs without discrimination to both downtown city dwellers and adventurers on remote mountain trails.

The easily accessible Lower Mainland region is home to numerous species of birds, while others winter here to escape the northern Arctic winds and snows, and still others stop to feed and rest during annual migrations.

In Vancouver, some elderly West End residents make a weekly ritual of greeting and feeding the ducks and swans around Lost Lagoon, on the fringe of Stanley Park. Park traffic sometimes stops to allow a gaggle of

Canada geese to cross the road. At the rocky cliffs near Siwash Rock, cormorants, gulls and guillemots make their nests, and within the forest bald eagles can be seen perched on tall trees.

Kingfishers and great blue herons are often seen hunting at Coal Harbour, Vancouver Island, along with loons, whose lonesome yodel symbolises the solitude of the Canadian wilderness.

Iona Island, in Richmond, is a good place to observe grebes, ducks, hawks, owls and passerines, while Pitt Meadows, in the Fraser Valley, is home to green herons, ducks, sandhill cranes, hawks and owls. But the best place for birdwatching is probably the **Reifel Bird Sanctuary**, located on the swampy, salty delta of the Fraser River. This area is home to Canada's largest concentration of waterfowl, including about 40,000 snow geese. The birds are best seen here from September to May.

Bird Alert (*tel: (250) 592 3381*) provides details of rare and unusual birds sighted in the Greater Vancouver area, or check online for rare bird sightings at *www.birding.bc.ca*

A bald eagle surveys his domain

Parksville

Nowhere in Canada does the ocean wash the shoreline so gently as it does along the popular sunny and sheltered bay at Parksville, the hub of Vancouver Island's east-coast 'Beach Country'. Today, about 45,000 people live in the triangle formed by Parksville and nearby Qualicum Beach and Coombs.

When Captain Vancouver explored the area two centuries ago, only Coast Salish Indians were living here. First settled in 1870, Parksville prospered steadily for many years with an economy based on forestry, tourism and farming. But in recent years development has been more spectacular, with large numbers of Canadians moving in to settle and to spend holidays enjoying the area's special attractions.

Little Qualicum Falls

Beaches and sandcastles

The waters of the Strait of Georgia flow in regularly twice a day along this coast. But whether the tide is in or out, there is ample space on the beach for a family outing or a solitary stroll.

Low tide leaves great expanses of hard, clean sand several hundred metres wide. This is the time when beachcombers come to hunt for oysters and dig for clams, local residents walk their dogs, and visitors and their children wade in the shallow pools, fly kites and build sandcastles.

The week-long Sandcastle Contest every August attracts master builders from around the world, and they have to work quickly to complete their creations in the damp sand while the tide is out. Another competition is held specially for the children (*tel: (250) 248 3613*).

At high tide, the hot summer sand warms the incoming water to a comfortable swimming temperature. Parksville beach claims the warmest outdoor swimming conditions in the province, with summer temperatures averaging 21°C (70°F). The shallow water provides an ideal waterpark where youngsters may safely swim, splash about, and ride dinghies and tubes.

The beach is probably at its most memorable in the early morning, when the loons are calling, the seals are barking and, across the water, the distant, deep mauve mountains are emerging against the orange sky.

South of Parksville, more than 2km (1¼ miles) of sandy shore also beckon at **Rathtrevor Beach Provincial**

Park (for reservations, call *(250) 474 1336*), one of the most popular family camping spots on Vancouver Island.

There are also 4km ($2^1/_2$ miles) of hiking trails frequented by deer and rabbits, dozens of picnic tables and barbecue pits, children's play areas, a nature house, an amphitheatre and, in summer, nature interpretative programmes.

Special area attractions

As a change from the beach, Paradise Adventure Golf (*tel: (250) 248 6612*), centrally located in Parksville, also offers fun for the whole family. The two 18-hole miniature courses have a fantasy setting, with a pirate galleon, Victorian mansion, watermill, lighthouse and bright floral displays.

For history lovers, **Craig Heritage Park and Museum** (*tel: (250) 248 6966*), 3km (2 miles) south of town, recalls the past with the 1912 Knox Church, the century-old French Creek post office, the McMillan loghouse, the Montrose school, a World War II fire station, and collections of late 19th-century clothing, old logging and farming equipment and early photographs of the area.

The Parksville coast is a birdwatchers' paradise, with its abundance of bald eagles, blue herons, loons, harlequin ducks and trumpeter swans.

Of the 57 species found here, 19 are on the North American birdwatchers' list of most keenly sought birds. One of

these is the Brent (Brant) goose, about 20,000 of which stop here during March and April to feed on the Pacific herring which spawns offshore, on the way to their Alaska nesting grounds. The event is celebrated every April during Parksville's Brant Wildlife Festival (*tel: (604) 924 9771, freephone (866) 288 7878; www.brantfestival.bc.ca*). The area is also a haven for anglers who come from far and wide to fish the waters.

Places to eat and stay

Accommodation for visitors in the Parksville-Qualicum Beach-Coombs area includes 1,500 hotel and motel units ranging from rustic cabins to modern condominiums and luxury beach resorts, with an additional 2,000 camping and recreational vehicle (RV) sites.

A range of fast-food and family eating places can be found along the Island Highway. There are also more elegant gourmet restaurants, including Cedar Room at Tigh-Na-Mara resort (*1095 East Island Highway, Parksville. Tel: (800) 663 7373; www.tigh-na-mara.com/index.htm*). Enjoy West Coast-inspired cuisine paired with BC's finest wines.

For further information on the Parksville-Qualicum Beach-Coombs area, contact the Parksville & District Chamber of Commerce, *PO Box 99, Parksville, BC V9P 2G3*, or visit: *www.chamber.parksville.bc.ca*

The tourism information office is about 3km (2 miles) south of Parksville (*tel: (250) 248 3613*).

Qualicum Beach

Qualicum Beach (*www.qualicum.bc.ca*) is a mecca for outdoor lovers and fishing enthusiasts. The Old School House (*tel: (250) 752 6133; www.theoldschoolhouse.org*), affectionately known as TOSH, is about 80 years old. It was renovated in the mid-1980s to house an art gallery with changing exhibits and eight studios with big viewing windows, so that visitors can watch resident artists at work.

Another interesting building, the Qualicum Heritage Inn, is housed in a former boarding school and sits on 2 hectares (5 acres) overlooking the ocean (*tel: (250) 752 9292; www.qualicumheritageinn.com*).

Numerous companies scattered along the coast offer charters of both powerboats and sailing boats, large and small. Travellers should contact the Parksville/Qualicum Beach Tourism Association (*tel: (250) 248 3613; www.chamber.parksville.bc.ca* or *www.visitparksvillequalicumbeach.com*).

Anglers flock to this area for the fighting coho, halibut and cod in the saltchuck around several offshore islands, and for the trout and steelhead in mountain streams and in the Big Qualicum, Little Qualicum and Englishman rivers.

Good golf courses in the neighbourhood include the Fairwinds (18 holes; *tel: (250) 468 7666*) on the Nanoose Peninsula, the Eaglecrest (18 holes; *tel: (250) 752 6311*) just south of Qualicum Beach, the Qualicum Beach Memorial (9 holes; *tel: (250) 752 6312*) on Crescent Road, and the Morningstar (18 holes; *tel: (250) 248 8161; www.golfvancouverisland.ca*) near the French Creek Marina.

Coombs

A ten-minute drive inland from Qualicum Beach, following Highway 4 to Port Alberni and Long Beach, is the tiny town of Coombs, instantly identifiable in summer by the goats grazing on the grass roof of the roadside Old Country Market. The surrounding cluster of shops sells everything from candied apples and antler carvings to sportswear. The Bluegrass Festival and Old Time Fiddlers' Contest held every summer attract country-and-western fans from all over the continent –

CATHEDRAL GROVE

About halfway along Highway 4, between Parksville and Port Alberni, stands Cathedral Grove, in MacMillan Park. Well-marked wilderness trails, carpeted with coniferous needles and cedar chips, meander through lush ferns, hemlocks, cedars and a grove of 800-year-old Douglas fir trees, which survived a forest fire 300 years ago. The largest tree measures 3m (10ft) in diameter and 9m (30ft) in circumference, and stands 75m (246ft) tall. Interpretative signs explain the woodland cycle of growth and decay. Little wonder this is called Cathedral Grove, for the elegant, moss-draped trees create a sanctuary as awe-inspiring as any ancient religious building in Europe.

probably a far cry from the demure, God-fearing colony intended when Salvation Army Commissioner Coombs led a dozen English families here to settle in 1910.

Nearby **Butterfly World** (Highway 4A; *tel: (250) 248 7026*) houses hundreds of exotic butterflies, representing 70 species, flying free in an enclosed tropical garden. Visitors can watch butterflies emerging from cocoons, flying, courting, sipping nectar, laying eggs or simply basking in the sunlight. Be sure to brush any butterflies off your shoulders before you leave.

A few kilometres further along the highway westward, Hillier's Sausage Factory (*tel: (250) 752 2390*) is an essential stop for campers and almost anyone else, since the European-style smoked meats made here are among the best in Canada.

Two provincial parks where outdoor lovers can walk, fish, swim, picnic or camp are also accessible from Coombs via Highway 4.

East of town, and some 16km south of the highway, is **Englishman River Falls Park**, with its impressive waterfall, gorges and pools set in forests of cedar, hemlock and fir trees.

Further west, on the way to Port Alberni, is **Little Qualicum Falls** with superb cataracts, pools and rocky chasms below Cameron Lake.

Coombs market with resident 'roof goats'

Port Alberni

Port Alberni, a town of some 20,000 people, is the gateway to Vancouver Island's spectacular west coast and Pacific Rim National Park. About a three-hour drive from Victoria, it lies at the head of the long saltwater Alberni Inlet, midway along scenic Highway 4, which crosses the island's rugged interior. Named after the Spanish explorer Pedro Alberni, who passed through the area two centuries ago, the town sprawls around the lumber yards and mills of the MacMillan Bloedel timber company.

The great outdoors offers adventure sports to suit all tastes

As the 'Salmon Capital of the World', Port Alberni is also a major fishing port, landing 20 per cent of BC's annual salmon catch from the 300 commercial fishing boats operating out of its harbour. Keen anglers flock here year-round to fish the salmon-rich waters of Alberni Inlet and nearby Barkley Sound. The most experienced especially enjoy Labour Day weekend here, when they compete in contests for more than $50,000 in prizes during the annual Clutesi Salmon Festival (Clutesi Haven Marina; *tel: (250) 724 6837*).

These competitions draw crowds to Alberni Harbour Quay, where the Clock Tower provides a panoramic view for miles around. Apart from the gift shops, art galleries, restaurants and boat companies offering cruises and fishing charters, the lively quayside offers live outdoor entertainment and rides on the little 'Two Spot' steam engine (*June–Sept*). The Quay is a great spot for visitors to mix and mingle, sample a meal or two, find a souvenir or watch the locals while sipping a drink at one of the outdoor cafés.

Port Alberni is a good base for various outdoor activities in the area. Nearby Mount Arrowsmith (1,800m/5,906 feet), which is snowcapped for most of the year, has a number of forest trails which are suitable for hiking in summer or skiing in winter. A half-hour drive south of town along a rough logging road is China Creek, a popular spot for windsurfers where skill-testing regattas are held every summer.
(*For more information see: www.city.port-alberni.bc.ca*)

Sproat Lake

Only a 15-minute drive west out of Port Alberni via Highway 4, the community of Sproat Lake borders the vast freshwater lake and provincial park of the same name. This is the home base of the Martin Mars water-bombers, the largest firefighting aircraft in the world, with tail-wing tips standing almost five storeys high. As they take off, these mammoth planes scoop up water from the lake to douse forest fires. Visitors are sometimes admitted to their land base, about a ten-minute walk east from the rustic Maples Resort on the north shore. But the planes are perhaps best seen from the deck of the Fish and Duck pub (*tel: (250) 724 4331*) as they become silhouettes against the setting sun.

One of the most dramatic rainforest walks in the world is the short and little-known, but marked, trail from the water-bomber base to Sproat Lake Park. From the campsites, picnic tables and boat-launching ramp in the park, it is another ten-minute walk east along the lakeshore to a floating dock from which some of the most interesting ancient petroglyphs on Vancouver Island can be viewed.

North of Sproat Lake, another intriguing place to visit is the **Robertson Creek Hatchery** (*tel: (250) 724 6521; open: daily 8am–4pm*) on the Stamp River, where millions of chinook, coho and steelhead are bred annually. Tours are available year-round, but the best time to visit is in September or October. During these months, the mature salmon return upstream after four years at sea and leap up a series of fish ladders in Stamp River Provincial Park (*tel: (250) 474 1336*) to spawn at their birthplace.

Sproat Lake is also a good jumping-off point for an exciting two- to four-day excursion that includes a canoe or water-taxi ride along the entire length of nearby **Great Central Lake**, followed by a 16km (10-mile) hike along a trail to the spectacular **Della Falls**. Plunging 444m (1,457 feet) in three magnificent cascades, the falls are among the highest in Canada.

Lady Rose

Gracious but hardworking, the MV *Lady Rose* (*tel: (250) 723 8313; www.ladyrosemarine.com*) is a sturdy 32m (105ft) long diesel packet, built

Della Falls

in Glasgow in 1937, and has been ferrying freight and passengers for over half a century. She is licensed to carry 100 passengers, and now offers visitors memorable sailing adventures. The MV *Frances Barkley* is a newer sister ship and takes over some of the destinations such as the Broken Island Group.

At 8am, a shrill blast announces departure from the Port Alberni quay for the voyage westward down Alberni Inlet to the Pacific Ocean. Passengers take breakfast or settle comfortably on the deck to enjoy the scenery. Dark forests rise sharply from the edges of the broad fiord. The ship sails along at a steady 12 knots past China Creek and then ties up at the floating post office dock in Kildonan to unload mail and

crates of goods. The next stops are at a couple of commercial fish farms, where groceries and pallets of fish food are delivered. Bald eagles circle overhead, hoping for left-overs. Then

A famous lady – *Lady Rose*

Sailing adventures await along the waterfront

the *Lady Rose* sails on to several isolated logging camps to unload mail and machinery parts.

In the summer (*June–Sept*), the *Frances Barkley* now takes visitors further north to the **Broken Islands Group**, in Barkley Sound. This cluster of about 100 small islands has several sheltered lagoons filled with sea birds and marine life that attract canoeists, kayakers and scuba divers. By noon the ship is docking at West Bamfield, where wooden boardwalks meander along the waterfront. As there is no road access here, water taxis cross the cove to East Bamfield, which is connected by a rough gravel logging road to Port Alberni. Accommodation is available for an overnight stay. Otherwise, the stopover time here may be from 40 minutes to 1½ hours.

The *Frances Barkley* also travels through the Broken Islands Group, stopping at the Sechart Whaling Station, to drop off and pick up wilderness lovers laden with backpacks and other sporting equipment. She then stops for about an hour at the fishing village of Ucluelet, before heading back up Alberni Inlet. The arrival back at Port Alberni is usually between 5.30pm and 6.30pm.

BC's lumber industry

The Pacific Northwest rainforests, among the most luxuriant in the world, contain trees more than 1,000 years old. More than half of BC is covered in forest, most of it on Crown land. To protect the resources for the future, a Forest Practices Code was established in June 1995.

The government grants tree-farming licences to logging companies, who are supposed to take care of the forest, clean up any waste and plant new trees. A dozen companies control more than 80 per cent of the provincial timber resources, and more than 90 per cent of the pulp mills and plywood plants. Until the 1980s, only about one-third of the cleared land was being reforested. Fortunately that is now changing, as more people are becoming increasingly aware of the

BC's forests are a major economic resource for the province and for Canada

Logs may be transported by rail, road or sea

necessity of preserving natural resources. Public protests are forcing forestry companies to take better care of the forests, with selective cutting and more planting.

The traditional lumberjack, in his long-sleeved checked shirt and heavy boots, has disappeared. The axe has been replaced by chainsaws, bulldozers, tree stumpers, hydraulic barkers, loaders, sorters and other machinery. In addition to loggers, the industry employs heavy-equipment operators, truck drivers, sawmill, pulp and paper-plant workers and tugboat captains.

After the chainsaws fell the trees, the branches are removed, and cranes move the logs to the roadside, where loading machines stack the logs onto trucks. The logs are then carried to a dumping ground and are sorted, measured and bundled. The biggest and best logs, such as the strong Douglas fir, go to plywood and other sawmills. Such smaller logs as western hemlock and balsam fir go to pulp and paper mills. Western red cedar, which is both weather- and rot-resistant, is often used for making roofing shales and shingles.

Pacific Rim National Park Reserve

No trip to Vancouver Island is complete without a visit to the wild and rugged Pacific Rim National Park Reserve on the western side of the island. Annual rainfall here averages 300cm (118in), so before setting out check *www.theweathernetwork.com/features/parks* or call *(250) 726 7721* for the weather forecast. The park is divided into three areas: from north to south, Long Beach, the Broken Islands Group and the West Coast Trail. More details at: *www.parkscan.harbour.com/pacrim*

Long Beach

Long Beach is accessible by car along a winding mountain highway from Port Alberni. Solitary walkers love this broad 11km (7-mile) long stretch of surf-swept sand, rocky outcrops and tidal pools. Big drift-logs, bull kelp and brilliant sea anemones and starfish dot the sands, where lucky beachcombers can occasionally pick up glass fishing floats, watermarked like sterling silver to identify the villages in Japan from where they came. When summer surf is up at Incinerator Rock, it is fun to watch surfers catching the waves ashore.

Drop in at the Wickaninnish Restaurant in Pacific Rim National Park for a signature espresso drink, or stay for dinner and admire the views of Vancouver Island's wild west coast. The restaurant also runs The Beachfront Café, a nice stop for a

warming snack (call for dinner reservations; *tel: (250) 726 7706*).

The two towns nearby, **Ucluelet** and **Tofino**, offer a variety of restaurants and accommodation. Tofino, surrounded by water on three sides, has several craft shops and art galleries. The Blue Heron (*tel: (250) 725 3277*) serves good seafood in an informal setting, and the Pacific Sands Beach Resort (*tel: (250) 725 3322, freephone (800) 565 BEACH; www.pacificsands.com*) has 60 rooms with balconies overlooking Cox Bay.

The West Coast Trail

Hardy hikers love the West Coast Trail, which meanders for 77km (48 miles)

WHALE WATCHING

Every spring from mid-March to mid-April, Pacific Rim National Park becomes a popular place for whale watching.

As their northbound migration reaches its peak, the 15-m (49-ft) long grey whales swim close to shore, often pausing to play in the coves and inlets along the coast.

Although whales are frequently sighted from rocky headlands along Long Beach, charter boat companies, such as **Jamie's Whaling Station** in Tofino (*tel: (250) 725 3919, freephone (800) 667 9913; www.jamies.com*) and **Remote Passages** (*tel: (250) 725 3330, freephone (800) 666 9833; www.remotepassages.com*), organise excursions.

The **Pacific Rim Whale Festival** at Tofino and Ucluelet (*tel: (250) 726 7798*) includes crab races, a gumboot golf tournament, concerts and plays.

The 'Whales in the Park' programmes include free guided whale-spotting hikes, lectures and films.

along an old telegraph route through wilderness rainforest, along sandstone cliffs and across slippery boardwalks in the southern part of **Pacific Rim National Park**. This rugged coastline was known as the graveyard of the Pacific for all the ships which sank off its shores.

The hike, which takes about a week to complete, is not for the faint-hearted. About a quarter of the hikers who set out do not manage to finish. But the challengers of this treacherous trail, accessible from mid-May to September only, are rewarded with the smell of the salty sea air; breathtaking views of undisturbed shoreline; occasional sightings of pods of whales and pudgy sea lions, and such sea birds as pigeon guillemots, marbled murrelets and pelagic cormorants; such treasures as Tsusiat Falls, where several cascades have created super swimming holes near the shore; and a campfire under the stars.

The trail runs from Port Renfrew (*tel: (250) 647 5434*) to Bamfield (*tel: (250) 728 3234*), or vice versa. To reserve, *tel: (250) 387 1642 or (604) 435 5622, or freephone 1 800-HELLO BC; www.hellobc.com. Park open: summer only; reservations required.*

Tofino in the Pacific Rim National Park Reserve

Tour: Sunshine Circle

Travellers trying to cram a lot into a two-week holiday in BC coastal country find a circular tour makes sense. This driving circuit includes four ferry rides (queues can be horrendous in summer) and covers the Sunshine Coast and eastern Vancouver Island (www.thesunshinecoast.com).

Allow 2 to 4 days.

Begin at Horseshoe Bay, a 30-minute drive northwest from downtown Vancouver, where BC Ferries (tel: 1 888 223 3779; www.bcferries.com) sail the 16km (10 miles) across Howe Sound to Langdale eight times a day.

1 Gibsons

From Langdale, a 3km (2-mile) long road winds west through forests and farmland along a craggy coastline to Gibsons, the gateway to the Sunshine Coast. Visitors like to tour Molly's Reach, the set where the television series *The Beachcombers*, the longest-running show in Canada, was filmed. Other options include a half-hour stroll

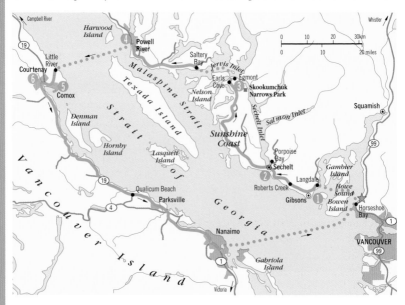

along the sea walk to a stone cairn marking the spot where Captain Vancouver landed two centuries ago, and studying the Salish native displays and the 25,000 seashells at the Sunshine Coast Museum. West of Gibsons, just off the main road, are good beaches and hiking trails. Nearby Roberts Creek, a community of artists and artisans, has a camping site right on the water's edge.

2 Sechelt

About 14km (8¾ miles) northwest of Gibsons stands Sechelt, the commercial centre of the Sunshine Coast. Abundant and colourful marine life entertains scuba divers. Delicacies of the deep are served at the Wharf Restaurants on Davis Bay and at the Blue Heron. The Tems Swiya Museum allows visitors to look back in time. The Sechelt natives, Canada's first self-governing aboriginal group, are renowned for fine carvings and woven cedar baskets.

3 Skookumchuk Narrows

Beyond Sechelt, an hour's hike from Egmont leads to lookouts above the Skookumchuk Narrows, where strong tides (highest during the summer and winter solstices) from three inlets rush at speeds of up to 15 knots through the spectacular rock-strewn passage. A ferry connects nearby Earls Cove with Saltery Bay across Jervis Inlet, where bald eagles fly overhead and playful killer whales, seals and sea lions compete for slow salmon. Divers can

see the bronze mermaid anchored 20m (66ft) down in Mermaid Cove.

4 Powell River

The next town, Powell River, offers the best salt- and freshwater fishing in Canada. The town has the large paper mill which produced Western Canada's first roll of newsprint in 1912.

5 Comox

Four ferries sail daily from Powell River to Comox (dock at Little River) on Vancouver Island, a 75-minute cruise west. Once known for coal mining, now fishing, forestry, farming and tourism sustain the Comox Valley. Visitors come for the sandy beaches, the local handicrafts and the biennial air show. The historic Filberg Lodge and Park is a good place to enjoy afternoon tea followed by a stroll in the gardens.

6 Courtenay

Another interesting place to walk is the adjacent town of Courtenay, where the downtown area has been remodelled with old-fashioned cobblestones and lamps, and brick planters brimming with flowers. The Courtenay Museum and Archives boasts the largest log cabin in the world, built in 1928, where displays of fossils, dolls and Indian artefacts recall times past.

Allow about two hours for the winding road following the coast south to Nanaimo, and the ferry which takes two hours to sail back to Horseshoe Bay.

Getting away from it all

Stretching in a great quadrangle between the 49th and 60th parallels, Canada's westernmost province brims with options for relaxation, recreation and adventure. Four times the size of Great Britain, BC's great outdoors covers 952,000sq km (367,569sq miles) of mountains and valleys, rivers and lakes, rainforests and deserts, coastlines and islands. Birdwatchers, kayakers and lovers of native Indian art and history like the Queen Charlottes for spotting such species as the rhinoceros auklet, paddling along calm inlets and studying moss-covered totems in abandoned villages.

The Pacific Ocean washes the shores of BC's main islands, Vancouver Island and the Haida Gwaii (Queen Charlottes). On Vancouver Island, Pacific Rim National Park lures whale watchers and other naturalists to wild beaches. Inland hikers explore the meadows of Forbidden Plateau and Strathcona Provincial Park and the first-growth rainforest in the Carmanah Valley. East of Vancouver, the terrain opens into the Okanagan Valley, where waterslides and wineries flank dude ranches and bird sanctuaries. The valley also has an abundance of apple, cherry and peach orchards. Further east, beyond the good hiking terrain of the Kootenays, stand the majestic Rocky Mountains, a mere 100 million years old, flanking the much older Purcell Mountains. The two became neighbours during the dinosaur era. The Burgess Shale site in **Yoho National Park** contains fossils from an ancient sea. More varieties of life are preserved here, in fantastic detail, than exist in all our modern oceans.

The high interior plateau of the Cariboo Chilcotin attracts equestrians, some of whom head out from the Sundance Guest Ranch on horseback to explore scenic trails, mountain meadows and river valleys. Canadian River Expeditions (*www.canriver.com*) offer a great 11-day circuit, which includes a boat cruise up the coast to Bute Inlet; a float-plane flight over the Homatho Icefield to turquoise Chilko Lake, and a day of fishing and hiking; an exciting raft trip along the Chilko, Chilcotin and Fraser rivers to the town of **Lillooet**; and a scenic return to Vancouver.

North of the Cariboo Chilcotin stretches big-game country. Stewart, Canada's most northerly ice-free port, has recorded up to 27m (89ft) of snowfall in one year. Winter lures visitors to explore the region by dog sledge and Skidoo and on nordic skis, while summer offers boating on **Atlin Lake**, rafting through icebergs on the great Tatshenshini River, and game spotting in Spatsizi Plateau Wilderness Provincial Park.

BC'S BEACHES

BC's 12,000km (7,458-mile) coastline, dotted with 6,500 islands, boasts lots of beaches, most suitable for sunning, swimming and beachcombing in summer. Vancouver Island is surrounded by beaches, and the Sunshine Coast sports its share, too.

One of the province's most treasured beaches, like many precious things, is fairly remote. Travel to the end of Highway 101 to Lund, north of Powell River on the Sunshine Coast, and take the 15-minute Lund water-taxi ride (*tel: (604) 483 9749*) to Savary Island. This crescent-shaped gem is ringed with long beaches, reminiscent of the South Pacific. A warm current mingles with the tides to produce summer waters reaching 22°C (72°F). When Captain Vancouver landed here in 1792, after a long voyage through the South Seas, he admired this island for 'beauty such as we have seldom enjoyed'. The pace of life has not changed much since. The three dozen permanent residents share Savary with many visitors, especially in summer. They come for the beautiful beaches, the warm waters and the many plants that normally grow much further south.

Near the government wharf, along 'Dough Row', windsurfers skim along with the breeze. Further away from human habitation, beachcombers find a variety of seashells, multicoloured rocks, and perfectly preserved sand dollars. Following the beaches around the island for about 30km (19 miles) is a full day's walk. The perfect way to end the day is with a bite to eat at the Mad Hatter Tea House, a five-minute walk from the government wharf. A sign nearby marks the trail to North America's largest arbutus tree. It takes four adults, arms stretched and touching at the fingertips, to circle the girth.

Visitors who want to linger longer will find a few rental cottages and B&Bs, but no formal campsites.

Getting away from it all

Quiet isolated locations are not hard to find

Overnighters who insist on sleeping on the beach are warned to watch for changing tides.

Boating

More than 250,000 BC households have boats. With so many waterways, boating seems as natural as driving. The choices are many and varied, ranging from a simple sunset dinner cruise around English Bay or a passive ride aboard a big BC ferry, to running the rapids of the mighty Fraser River or fishing offshore with whales, sea lions and cormorants for company.

Desolation Sound

Lund, on the Sunshine Coast (*see p127* for how to get there), and Campbell River, on eastern Vancouver Island, are good starting points for Desolation Sound, 32km (20 miles) north of Powell River. The largest of BC's 32 marine parks, Desolation Sound offers protected warm waters backed by coastal mountains. Native pictographs and coastal lakes make trips ashore interesting, and the waters provide fresh oysters and salmon for dinner.

Okanagan Lake

Okanagan Lake is located in the Okanagan Valley of BC. The lake is neat and clear, 150km (93 miles) long and 300m (984ft) deep. It is surrounded by mountains and several communities, the largest being Kelowna.

Okanagan Lake has become a popular venue for waterskiing, boating, houseboating and sunbathing at the many surrounding beaches.

It is also home to the Ogopogo, a legend in the Okanagan, which attracts many people from around the world who attempt to capture this 'friendly serpent' on film.

Princess Louisa Inlet

Jervis Inlet, further south on the Sunshine Coast, leads to Princess Louisa Inlet, one of the most scenic fiords in the world. Bordered by craggy granite cliffs streaked with waterfalls and capped with evergreens, the fiord is home to many sea mammals and birds. Erle Stanley Gardner said it best: 'There is no use in describing that inlet. Perhaps an atheist could view it and remain an atheist, but I doubt it.' On top of the gorge is a marine park, crowned by the 40m (131ft) high Chatterbox Falls.

The Gulf Islands

Sailing the sheltered waters of the Gulf Islands is also great fun. But watch for 'deadheads', mostly submerged waterlogged tree trunks which have escaped from log booms and could grind your vessel to an untimely halt. Some boat rental companies offer weekend flotilla charters, in which a group of boats sails in the company of a mother ship skippered by a certified instructor. The instructor does the navigating, thus enabling out-of-towners to explore unknown waters with ease. Courses are also offered in basic coastal cruising, coastal navigation, advanced sailing, celestial navigation and offshore sailing.

The Bowron Lakes Circuit

The quietest and most relaxing boating adventure may be the Bowron Lakes circuit, named one of the top ten canoe trips in the world by *Outside Magazine.* Deep in the heart of the Cariboo Mountains west of the Rockies, this rectangular chain of lakes and connecting waterways is set within a 121,600-hectare (300,470-acre) wilderness park. Along the 116km (72-mile) route, the placid blue waters reflect glacier-streaked mountains rising to 2,100m (6,890ft). The region is home to many birds and such other wildlife as moose, bear, lynx and beaver. Paddlers set off from Bowron Lake Lodge and Becker's Lodge, where a variety of canoes and camping gear can be rented. The circuit can be canoed any time from June to October, although June seems to be the best month for seeing both birds and other wildlife.

Shuswap Lake

For a totally different boating holiday, head for the interior town of **Sicamous**, on the Trans-Canada Highway west of Revelstoke. Here, visitors can rent a houseboat, complete with a hot tub on the deck, take the wheel, and head out to tie up at one of 14 beaches on Shuswap Lake. The houseboats are simple to manoeuvre and great fun for families. Houseboaters can swim, fish, and explore the area beneath the Shuswap Highlands from their floating home.
See www.shuswap.bc.ca for information and for places to rent houseboats.

The Atlin Lake Wilderness

For a boating adventure in the true north, head for Atlin, which lies near the BC/Yukon border. Atlin Lake, which is 100km (62 miles) long, is the place to be in midsummer when the sun rises at 4.30am and sets at 11.15pm, leaving enough light to take midnight photos. Houseboaters, paddlers and sailors can also go ashore to hike, look for mountain goats, bathe in hot springs and admire alpine scenery.

The best way to get there is to fly to Whitehorse in the Yukon, and rent a car or catch the Atlin Express bus for the three-hour ride south.

If you go

Request the *BC Outdoor & Adventure Guide* and *Charter Boat Adventure* brochures from Tourism BC or any BC Travel InfoCentre. Pathways Tours (*tel: (604) 514 8024, freephone (800) 924 2944; www.bowronlakes.com*) organises

In BC, boating is almost as popular as driving

Getting away from it all

canoeing tours through the Bowron Lakes for novice paddlers.

Call Yukon Tourism in Whitehorse (*tel: (800) 661 0494; www.touryukon.com*) for information on trips to and on Atlin Lake.

Running the rapids

Suddenly a menacing sound rumbles ahead. There is no turning back now. 'Hang on tight!' shouts the boatman. The big rubber raft careens through the foaming rapids. White water slams the pontoons, then gracefully sprays up and falls, and the raft plunges with the flow downstream to calmer waters.

This is rapid-running, but on such chauffeured expeditions, skilled rapid-runners man the oars. The rafts are not easy to capsize, but passengers wear life jackets, just in case. In rough water, the raft may buck and leap like a Wild West bronco. River-running is not always a dry experience, so it is best to keep cameras in waterproof bags.

River-running is more than just navigating rivers. Most trips allow time for hikes ashore and a cooling swim in the river. On longer trips, the boatmen may become chefs and grill salmon steaks or hamburgers over an open fire, while the aroma of freshly brewed coffee fills the air. Often a happy evening can be spent around a campfire chatting with new-found friends, with time left over to gaze at the moon and stars before settling in for the night.

The mighty Fraser River

Several powerful rivers surge through BC, carrying such Indian names as Chilko and Chehalis (meaning 'where the chest of a canoe grounds on a sandbar'), and honouring such early explorers as Thompson and Fraser. But the Fraser River is the greatest of them all.

Rising as a trickle in the southeast corner of Mount Robson Provincial Park in the Rockies, the Fraser travels 1,280km (795 miles) southwest to empty into the Pacific. From Mount Robson, the river flows fast and pristine to Quesnel, where the blue waters turn turgid brown, due, at least in part, to chemical waste of pulp mills. There are rapids at Scuzzy Rock, China Bar and **Hell's Gate** – appropriately named, for here the mighty Fraser churns through a narrow, glacially carved 34m (112ft) wide gorge. As the raft runs from Boston Bar for 42km (26 miles) down to Yale, the boatman usually

---

SIMON FRASER

Simon Fraser was an American-born fur trader and explorer for the North West Company. He was also one of the great river-runners of the 19th century.

In 1808, against the advice of the native Indians, he led an expedition in birch-bark canoes down a river he believed to be the Columbia. He was mistaken, and that fast river of many rapids and deep gorges now bears his name.

At Hell's Gate, Fraser wrote: 'It is so wild that I cannot find words to describe our situation at times … a desperate undertaking!'

His persistent and perilous journey changed the map of the continent.

Rafters need skill and courage to brave the rapids

gives a running commentary on the mining history of the area.

For a more gentle trip, boaters start at Hope and wend their way past New Westminster to the Oak Street Bridge in Vancouver. This shows how the city is developing close to the river.

The Creston Valley

Another gentle journey is the one- to three-day canoe trip through the Creston Valley (*www.crestonvalley.com*). Paddlers start at the Canada/US border on Highway 21 and go north with the flow to Kootenay Lake. Protected marshlands make for safe canoeing.

More than 250 species of birds inhabit or visit the valley, and the area between Creston and Nelson is home to 140 pairs of osprey, one of the largest osprey nesting sites in the world.

Contact the Creston Valley Wildlife Management Centre (*tel: (250) 402 6900; www.crestonwildlife.ca*) for more canoeing information.

The Chilko River

Another exciting rafting trip follows the Chilko River. The run is gentle from Chilko Lake to Lava Canyon, where sets of grade-five rapids await the rafter. The last stretch runs from the Taseko River junction to the Chilcotin River junction. *www.chilcotin.bc.ca*

Chilliwack River Rafting Adventures
Tel: freephone 1 800 410 7238; www.chilliwackriverrafting.com
Fraser River Raft Expeditions Ltd
Tel: (800) 363 RAFT; www.fraserraft.com

Getting away from it all

Hyak Wilderness Adventures
Tel: (604) 734 8622, freephone (800) 663 RAFT; www.hyak.com

Kumsheen Raft Adventures
Tel: (250) 455 2296, freephone (800) 663 6667; www.kumsheen.com

Whistler River Adventures
Tel: (604) 932 3532, freephone (888) 932 3532; www.whistlerriver.com

Riding the rails

A few years ago, the *Pacific Coast Starlight*, the *Cariboo Prospector* and the *Whistler Northwind* were gone in one fell swoop when BC Rail ceased to exist. But rail travel is so much a part of BC's history and soul that new journeys were bound to loom on the horizon before long. And so they have: in 2006, the *Whistler Mountaineer* was launched, a spanking new three-hour rail trip along the 'Sea-to-Sky' route that follows the coastline from Vancouver to Whistler. Like its very successful parent, the *Rocky Mountaineer* that runs from Vancouver to Banff and Jasper, the *Whistler Mountaineer* offers the finest in local cuisine served against the panoramic mountain and coastal scenery.

Operated by Rocky Mountaineer Vacations (*tel: (877) 460 3200; www.rockymountaineer.com*), the 'old timer' *Rocky Mountaineer* ride through British Columbia to the Rockies has been dubbed one of the most spectacular rail tours in the world. Passengers return again and again to enjoy the dramatic journey. Although the trip could be done in a day, the *Rocky Mountaineer* takes two days so that passengers can soak in the maximum eye-popping views during daylight hours. On the first day, the biggest 'wows' come through the Fraser Canyon; on the second day, it's the Rockies. On-board entertainment is part of the ride, but the best bit is the running commentary by staff members who pride themselves on knowing absolutely everything and delivering their facts with humour and drama. During the journey, lush rainforests are punctuated by deep canyons and raging waterfalls. There are lakes and forests, painted deserts, dramatic bridges high above rivers, tunnels, glaciers and soaring mountain peaks. Most people opt to do the trip during the spring, summer and autumn months but there's also a winter ride into the Rockies through the Land of a Million Christmas Trees. It's rumoured Santa even comes on board.

Vancouver is also the Western terminus for VIA Rail's *Canadian*, a continuous trip from the coast to Toronto, taking in the full panorama of Canada's distinct geographic changes. Seeing the country with VIA is a once-in-a-lifetime dream for many visitors. VIA's *Skeena* also follows a northerly route across the middle of the province from Prince Rupert to Jasper.

Riding the trails

Horse riding is an easy and pleasant way to explore BC outdoors. Riding appeals to almost all ages: the views can be marvellous, the pace therapeutic and the environmental impact minimal. Because the animals carry the gear, horseback holidays have extra appeal for families with young children who might find arduous hikes overwhelming. Most BC outfitters and dude ranchers use placid quarter horses and Arabian stock for trekking. They have comfortable gaits and respond to neck reining, which allows one hand free to hang on to the saddle horn.

In the Lower Mainland, latent cowpokes can canter in Golden Ears Park. Professional stables guide riders out of Maple Ridge

Horse riding is a great way to explore BC

(*www.mapleridge.com*) for a day trek to Alouette Lake, where they can hitch their horses to a tree and go for a swim. Several hundred kilometres of trails in **Manning Park** (*www.manningparkresort.com*) are ideal for ambling through Canada's mountainous west. Late summer or autumn is a good season to ride, as the insects retreat and the autumn leaves turn bright red, rust and yellow. In mid-September at Manning, the alpine larch trees on Frosty Mountain turn a deep gold before dropping their deciduous needles.

North of Vancouver, at **Williams Lake** (*www.williamslake.ca*), riders can head west to **Tatlayoko Lake** in the Chilcotin for week-long journeys to see ice caves, fossil beds and meadows where grizzly bears forage in the Potato Mountain Coast Range. East of Williams Lake, riders can overnight at Helmcken Falls Lodge (*tel: (250) 674 3657; www.helmckenfalls.com*) near Clearwater and ride lodge horses along the trails of Wells Gray Park.

For unusual trekking, try remote **Mount Edziza Park** (contact the Skeena District in Smithers, *tel: (250) 847 7320*), where the Tahtlan Indians introduce riders to moonscapes of cinder cones and mountains of shale, occasionally pockmarked by hungry grizzlies hunting gophers. Any saddle sores suffered during the long trek may be soothed by hellebore root, which the guide boils up in an old tin can.

The iron horse

The history of the railway in Canada is the history of the development of this sprawling, rugged land. The CPR was founded in 1881 and it took 54 months to complete. The last spike was driven in Craigellachie, BC, in 1885. The line connects Montreal with Port Moody, BC, a distance of 4,627km (2,876 miles).

Where the iron horse ambled, settlers and prosperity usually followed. The first scheduled passenger train arrived in Vancouver in 1887. The arrival of the railway energised the economy of the Pacific Northwest, bringing large numbers of Canadians and Europeans. The population of Vancouver mushroomed from 900 to 8,000 within five years, and the Canadian Pacific Railway (*www.cprheritage.com*) became the city's largest employer.

The CPR built the first Hotel Vancouver, bought and sold land, operated sternwheelers on BC rivers and ran steamships across the Pacific Ocean. Freight trains running across the country encouraged the exploitation of natural resources. Such BC products as fur, coal, timber, gold and fish suddenly found accessible markets.

The transcontinental train service has been curtailed in recent years, since cars and trucks, along with aircraft and helicopters, have diminished passenger demand. Most British Columbians now drive or fly to get from one place to another, but holidaymakers still love the romance and the rattle of the rails, the gentle pace, and the friendliness of the conductors and other passengers from all over the world.

Thundering past snowcapped mountains

CPR tracks run through some remarkable scenery

Yet the scenery remains the greatest attraction. Early CPR President Cornelius Van Horne commented back in 1895, 'Since we cannot export the scenery, we shall have to import the tourists'. Rail travellers love the stillness and splendour of the unfolding wilderness panorama of mountains, canyons, lakes, rivers, streams, forests and rolling ranchlands, and glimpses of such elusive wildlife as deer, elk, moose, bighorn sheep and bear. They love the dramatic spiral tunnel near Kicking Horse Pass; the geography lesson, and whistle stops at remote towns and villages; and the sense of pioneer adventure.

Some useful websites giving information on scenic tours across Canada are: *www.cprtours.com*, *www.viarail.ca* and *www.rkymtnrail.com*

Provincial parks

There are more than 450 provincial parks in BC, encompassing glaciers, grasslands, rainforests, rivers, lakes, dormant volcanoes, mountains, islands, fiords and beaches. There are over 2,000km (1,243 miles) of hiking trails, and more than 90 parks with good canoeing and hiking, some with good fishing and some with boat launches. More than 12,000 pitches in 175 campsites are scattered throughout the parks. Several have interpretative programmes, so visitors can hear talks about flora and fauna and star-gaze with astronomers. Parks cover more than 5 per cent of BC, an area larger than the province of Nova Scotia. For more information contact BC Parks at *(800) 689 9025* or, in Vancouver, *(604) 689 9025*.

Mount Robson Provincial Park

A favourite with many adventurers, Mount Robson Provincial Park contains the highest peak (3,954m/12,972ft) in the Canadian Rockies, the headwaters of the Fraser River and spectacular scenery, but has limited access. From June to September, visitors admire more than 50 species of alpine flowers, 170 species of birds (including golden eagles), grizzly bears, caribou, mountain goats and hoary marmots. Robson Helimagic (*tel: (250) 566 4700, freephone (877) 454 4700; www.robsonhelimagic.com*) runs heli-hikes into the park for people of all ages. The base camp, at 2,073m (6,801ft), nestles in a rain shadow surrounded by flowering meadows and snowy peaks.

Pure water flows in glacier-fed streams. Hikers bathe downstream in natural pools and waterfalls, and spend about six hours each day exploring the wilderness. After an evening slide show in the main mess tent, the Northern Lights sometimes brighten the darkening sky (*www.mountrobsonlodge.com*).

Strathcona Park

BC's oldest park boasts six of the seven highest peaks on Vancouver Island, along with the Comox Glacier, the island's last remaining icefield, thus earning the nickname 'Little Switzerland'. Although Strathcona is truly a wilderness park, day trippers take the half-hour drive west from Courtenay in the Comox Valley in summer to enjoy the alpine flowers and hike the Forbidden Plateau.

Available accommodation includes campsites at Buttle Lake and Ralph River, and the Strathcona Lodge (*tel: (250) 286 3122; www.strathcona.bc.ca*), on the lake just outside the park. The lodge's superb outdoor education centre offers apprenticeships in wilderness leadership, rock climbing, mountaineering, white-water canoeing, kayaking and photographing wildlife. Experienced hikers enjoy the Flower Ridge, Elk River and Marble Meadows trails radiating out from Buttle Lake, as well as the challenge of scaling the

2,200-m (7,218-ft) Golden Hinde. Della Falls, the continent's highest at 440m (1,444ft), are located in the southern part of the park. Visitors take a water-taxi from the Ark Resort (*tel: (250) 723 2657; www.arkresort.com*) near Port Alberni up Great Central Lake and then hike 16km (10 miles) to the falls (*www.strathconapark.com*).

Tweedsmuir Provincial Park
This is BC's largest park. Many overseas visitors rent campers in Vancouver, drive north to Williams Lake on the Cariboo Highway (97), and then west on the Freedom Highway (20) to Bella Coola. This route runs through southern Tweedsmuir Park. Hair-raising switchbacks lead down into the **Atnarko River Valley**, a good location for day hikes into the Rainbow Mountains.

The Rainbow Mountain Outfitting (*tel: (250) 742 3539; www.rainbowadventuresbc.com*) of Anahim Lake, guides in these parts for three generations, come highly recommended for week-long horseback outings during July and August. The Hunlen Lakes area, which provides excellent canoeing, is where the pioneer settler Ralph Edwards helped save trumpeter swans from extinction during the 1950s. Ralph's son John runs the Hunlen Wilderness Camp.

Wells Gray Provincial Park
Considered one of BC's finest parks, it is located just north of Clearwater, a

five-hour drive north from Vancouver on Highway 5. The park offers great hiking in summer and hut-to-hut skiing in winter. Clearwater Lake is easily accessible and offers good beaches and good fishing. In winter, the 142m (466ft) Helmcken Falls freeze into a 20-storey ice cone, broader at the base than a football field. Helmcken Falls Lodge (*tel: (250) 674 3657; www.helmckenfalls.com*) was originally built as a hunting lodge at the entrance to the park. Visitors love it as a base for hiking, canoeing, backpacking, horse riding, mountaineering, glacier exploration and fishing.
Thompson River District.
Tel: (250) 851 3000.

Waterfalls appear beside the road, here between Ucluelet and Tofino

The Rockies

This mountainous region of outstanding scenic splendour stretches northwest for 1,400km (870 miles) along the BC-Alberta border. It is bounded on the east by vast prairies and on the west by the Rocky Mountain Trench, one of the longest valleys in the world. Most of the Rocky Mountains are in Alberta. For much of their length, they form the Continental Divide separating Canada's east- and west-flowing rivers.

Mount Robson, the highest peak, shoots nearly 4,000m (13,120ft) skyward, while Mount Assiniboine, the Matterhorn of Canada, is a breathtaking 3,600m (11,811ft) tusk of layered rock carved into a pyramid shape by glacial cirques.

The Rockies were created about 65 million years ago, when the land uplifted and broke along great fault lines, forcing the rock to fold and buckle. During the last Ice Age, about 12,000 years ago, glaciers completed this sculpting by nature.

The Kootenay Indians have lived here for 10,000 years. As hunters and gatherers, they knew all the secret passes through the mountains. When the explorer and fur trader David Thompson eventually struggled through Howes Pass in 1807, the Kootenays nicknamed him 'Star Man'.

Although other explorers and traders, prospectors, missionaries and homesteaders (pioneer farmers) followed, few settled. The discovery of gold at Wild Horse Creek in 1863 brought a surge of 5,000 souls, but when the gold was gone only about 20 families remained. Two decades later, the Northwest Mounted Police established a detachment here, headed by Superintendent Samuel Steele.

Today, the area is a haven for the adventure tourist, who heads here in passionate pursuit of the peaks and the outdoor action. The air is fresh, the waters clear and the scenery awesome. From such guest ranches as Top of the World, Beaverfoot and Bull River, visitors can canter around the countryside all day and return to find freshly caught rainbow trout sizzling on the grill. Others may prefer to hike over alpine meadows, play golf or paddle, sail, windsurf or waterski on emerald lakes. Or they may savour the silvery cascades of Laughing Falls, or soak in warmer water at the Radium, Fairmont or Lussin hot springs.

Wildlife watchers, especially at dawn and dusk, may spot moose, deer, elk, mountain goat, bear, lynx, coyote and marmots. Winter resorts offer nordic and alpine skiing, while heli-skiing (helicopter skiing) in the Bugaboo area is an experience of a lifetime.

Fort Steele

At this fine historic heritage town, the gold-mining past is vividly present in over 60 reconstructed buildings. Highlights include ice-cream making, stagecoach rides, recreated old newspapers, Victorian vaudeville at the Wildhorse Theatre and workers costumed as blacksmiths, carpenters, quilters and weavers.

The town is 16km (10 miles) northeast of Cranbrook. Tel: (250) 426 7352, 24-hour hotline. Open: daily sunrise–sunset. Admission charge.

Kimberley

Canada's highest city at 1,117m (3,665ft), Kimberley is nicknamed the 'Bavarian City of the Rockies'. The red-brick pedestrian Platzl holds the world's largest operating cuckoo clock. Bavarian-style buildings sport dark wood panelling, floral decorations and window boxes filled with red geraniums. European delis and restaurants serve such German specialities as *Weisswurst*, *Spetzle* and *Strudel*. Kimberley has been a zinc-, silver- and lead-mining town since the 1890s. A 20-minute train ride carries visitors in an old mining car through a tunnel and over a trestle.

For information on accommodation, tel: (250) 427 3922, freephone (800) 667 0871; www.kimberleyvacations.bc.ca

Kootenay National Park

Here, a half-hour hike through moss-carpeted forest leads to the Paint Pots, ponds stained red, orange and yellow by iron oxide which the Kootenay Indians used for body and rock painting.

Located south of Yoho National Park. Open: year-round. Tel: (250) 343 6783.

Yoho National Park

With 28 peaks more than 3,000m (9,843ft) high, all layered with rock, blue ice and snow, this park offers such varied sights as the Takakkaw Falls, the spiral railway tunnels leading up to Kicking Horse Pass and the Burgess Shale fossil beds, which include petrified remains of 120 species, dating as far back as 530 million years.

Located just west of the Continental Divide and Banff National Park. Open: year-round.

Banff and Jasper National Park (Alberta)

Canada's oldest national park, Banff was established in 1885 after hot springs were seen gushing from the side of Sulphur Mountain. The main resort towns are Banff, named after Banffshire in Scotland, and Lake Louise, located at the Continental Divide.

Jasper National Park, the largest designated parkland in the Rocky Mountains, lies north of Banff and west of Edmonton. Scenic highlights include Mount Edith Cavell and Maligne Lake, a large and beautiful remnant of a retreating glacier. The Columbia Icefield, a glacier that has not yet retreated, is about an hour's drive south (*see www.banff.com*).

For further information, contact Kootenay Rockies Tourism at *(250) 427 3344* or *www.kootenayrockies.com*

Shopping

Western Canadians have been shopping in Vancouver ever since the Oppenheimer brothers began outfitting prospectors and homesteaders more than a century ago. The range of goods has, of course, expanded far beyond the dreams of those early settlers, and sturdy outdoor clothing is as much a fashion item as a necessity these days.

The high standard of living and high expectations of its citizens have made Vancouver a wonderful place to shop – and prices are often lower than in Europe. There are shops everywhere, from the heritage areas of Gastown to the modern, underground Pacific Centre mall; from the colourful markets to the trendy designer boutiques.

In addition to all the usual shopping mall and high-street retailers, there are specialist stores for just about everything: items for left-handed people, clothes for short or tall people, shoes for big feet, pewterware, cigars, artistic chocolates, etc.

The eclectic range of goods is also broadened by the diverse cultures of the immigrant populations.

Robson Street is the hub of it all – the most popular strolling street in Vancouver – where people meet and greet, gaze at store windows filled with clothes and curios from around the globe, and linger in the cafés and restaurants to watch the world go by.

On Friday evenings in summer, there is open-air ballroom dancing to live music in Robson Square (*tel: (604) 925 5003*). The other main shopping streets are Water Street in Gastown, Pender Street in Chinatown and South Granville Street for art, antiques and carpets.

Arts and crafts

Canoe Pass Gallery

The work of gifted Canadian Native artists is on display in this heritage-village gallery, including masks, carvings, prints, jewellery and sculpture. *3866 Bayview St, Steveston. Tel: (604) 272 0095.*

Coastal Peoples Fine Arts Gallery

Native artwork, including gold and silver jewellery, masks, totem poles, paintings, prints and Inuit sculptures. *1072 Mainland St, Yaletown. Tel: (604) 685 9298.*

Crafthouse

The gallery of the Crafts Association of British Columbia, with items chosen to

represent a spirit of exploration and a tradition of quality.
1386 Cartwright St, Granville Island. Tel: (604) 687 7270.

Hill's Native Art
An enormous selection of native art and craft work.
165 Water St, Gastown. Tel: (604) 685 4249. Also at 1008 Government St, Victoria (tel: (604) 385 3911); and at 76 Bastion St, Nanaimo (tel: (604) 755 7873).

Khot-la-cha
Authentic Coast Salish handicrafts on sale include carvings, moose-hide crafts, clothing and porcupine-quill jewellery.
270 Whonoak St, North Vancouver. Tel: (604) 987 3339.

Object Design
Jewellery, photography, wood and glass by local contemporary artists. In the Creekhouse building on Granville Island.
1551 Johnston St. Tel: (604) 683 7763.

Trading Post
Native artists still come to this restored 1911 log cabin near the famous Capilano suspension bridge to sell their work. Items include spirit masks, jewellery, knitwear and leatherware.
3735 Capilano Rd, North Vancouver. Tel: (604) 985 7474. Open: daily.

Clothing
Angel
The clothing here is described as 'wearable art', with hand-painted garments for children and adults.
2 Powell St. Tel: (604) 681 0947.

Diana Sanderson Studio
Fine quality, hand-dyed and woven silk clothing, accessories and jewellery.
1551 Johnston St, Granville Island. Tel: (604) 687 7455.

Dream Apparel & Articles For People
Locally designed hip and comfortable urban wear in Gastown.
311 West Cordova St. Tel: (604) 683 7326.

The fragrance of fresh fruit can be intoxicating at Granville Island's public market

Hunt and Gather

Clothing, accessories and handbags, all made right in this Carrall Street shop, known for its incredible retail space.
225 Carrall St. Tel: (604) 633 9559.

Leather Ranch

A huge selection of quality leather and suede fashions and accessories.
In Victoria at 1150 Douglas Street.

OK Boot Corral

Western boots, hats, belts, buckles, bolo ties and souvenirs of the old west.
205 Carrall St, Gastown.
Tel: (604) 684 BOOT (2668).

Repp Big and Tall

Casual and smart clothing for big, tall guys, with tailoring available on the premises for quick alterations.
475 West Hastings St. Tel: (604) 681 3548. Open: Mon–Sat 9am–5.30pm; Sun noon–5pm.

Roots Canada

Established in 1973, Roots now has more than 80 stores across the country, selling its own line of rugged, casual clothing for the family, including leather jackets, outerwear, footwear and athletic wear.
Pacific Centre, 701 West Georgia St. Tel: (604) 408 4250. Also at 1001 Robson at Burrard St (tel: (604) 683 4305); and Metrotown Centre, Burnaby (tel: (604) 435 5554).

Tall Girl

This store offers fashion, sportswear, footwear, lingerie and sleepwear, in a range of sizes all designed for tall, long-waisted or long-legged figures.
644 Hornby St. Tel: (604) 688 9238.

Shopping for those with a sweet tooth on fashionable Robson Street

Also at 1209 Douglas St, Victoria (tel: (250) 388 7034).

Tilley Endurables

Travel and adventure clothing, including the famous Tilley hat – it floats, ties on, repels rain, won't shrink and comes with a lifetime guarantee and a four-page owner's manual!
2401 Granville St & 8th St.
Tel: (604) 732 4287. Open: Mon–Sat 10am–5.30pm, Sun noon–5pm.

True Value Vintage Clothing

You can buy, sell, trade and hire vintage clothing here, or you can just browse around the range of garments and accessories from the 1920s to the '70s.
710 Robson St. Tel: (604) 685 5403.

Duty-free shopping

Tourists are eligible for a rebate on certain goods that will be taken outside the country within 60 days of purchase. The easiest way to benefit from the scheme is to shop at a duty-free outlet, where instant reductions of up to 60 per cent are available on the price of qualifying items, including spirits, cigarettes, perfume, cosmetics and designer merchandise. Otherwise, you have to wait until you get home before applying for the rebate. Information is available at duty-free outlets.

Spirit of the North Duty Free

1026 Alberni St, Vancouver. Tel: (604) 683 2416.

Gifts, souvenirs and specialist stores

Accent on Pewter

A vast selection of pewtercraft, including jewellery and tableware.
1289 Robson St. Tel: (604) 683 5799. Open: daily 10am–6pm (9pm Thur & 10pm Fri), Sun noon–6pm.

Chackas

Housewares, accessories, jewellery, bags and the coolest in cocktail shakers.
Tel: (604) 681 6730.

Chocolate Arts

Chocolate medallions with Haida designs.
2037 West 4th Ave. Tel: (604) 739 0475. Open: Mon–Sat 10am–6pm, Sun noon–5pm.

Crash

Contemporary home furnishings for the spacially challenged.
1551 Johnston St. Tel: (604) 684 9922. Open: daily 9.30am–6pm.

Grand Maple

Quality Canadian souvenirs, including a large collection of BC jade and, of course, maple syrup.
1046 Robson St. Tel: (604) 681 8979.

Industrial Artifacts

One-of-a-kind furniture, vases, candleholders, lighting and home décor, fashioned from recycled industrial materials.
49 Powell Street. Tel: (604) 874 7797.

Lululemon Athletica

Trendy yoga apparel with a designer West Coast twist.
1148 Robson St. Tel: (604) 681 3118; www.lululemon.com

Shoppers can browse well into the evening

A street stall in Chinatown

New-Small and Sterling
Functional and decorative contemporary glass designs.
1440 Old Bridge Street on Granville Island. Tel: (604) 681 6730.

The Umbrella Shop
Now into its third generation, this family business has an in-house factory making a large selection of umbrellas to complement the imported ones.
1106 W Broadway. Tel: (604) 669 9444. Open: Mon–Fri 9.30am–5.30pm, Sat 10am–5pm.

Markets
Vancouver's markets are lively and entertaining places to shop. In a party atmosphere of street entertainment and fast food, you can browse around stalls selling Canadian crafts, souvenirs, designer kitchenware, flowers and all kinds of fresh produce.

Granville Island Market
The oldest of several waterfront markets, this one is on a broad outdoor deck overlooking the marine activity in False Creek.
On Granville Island; accessible by AquaBus (tel: (604) 689 5858) from the foot of Granville St. Open: Tue–Sun 9am–6pm.

Lonsdale Quay Market
Highlights among the wide selections of goods available are The Forest Studio for gems and stones, and Allyado for luggage and travel goods.
123 Carrie Cates Court, North Vancouver; accessible by SeaBus from downtown. Tel: (604) 985 6261. Open: daily 9.30am–6.30pm (9pm on Fri).

Park Royal Market
Visiting Park Royal is like doing a tour of Europe, with its Belgian bakery, German deli, Italian pasta outlets, Scottish butcher and international news-stand.
Park Royal South, Marine Drive, West Vancouver. Tel: (604) 922 3211. Open: Mon–Sat 9.30am–5.30pm (9pm on Thur & Fri), Sun noon–6pm.

Robson Market
On the upstairs level, artisan-vendors and a cluster of cafés have the impressive backdrop of a 43m (141ft) long mural depicting life in the West End – all overlooking the colourful displays of produce below.

1610 Robson St. Tel: (604) 682 2733.
Open: daily 9am–9pm.

Vancouver Flea Market

Over 360 stalls vie for business
in the city's largest flea market,
where you can bargain for unusual
souvenirs.

703 Terminal Ave, five-minute walk from
Main St. Tel: (604) 685 0666.
Open: Sat–Sun & holidays 9am–5pm.

Westminster Quay Market

Getting here is half the fun, involving
a spectacular 30-minute ride by
SkyTrain from downtown. The market
overlooks the Fraser River.

810 Quayside. Tel: (604) 520 3881.
Open: daily 9.30am–6.30pm.

Shopping malls

The Landing

This beautifully restored heritage
building houses an exceptional
range of elegant fashion stores and
speciality goods, and a selection
of fine restaurants.

375 Water St. Tel: (604) 483 5050.

Granville Island Market beside False Creek

Landsdowne Park

Five minutes' drive from the airport, this mall has over 120 shops, including department stores, designer fashions and many speciality shops. There is also an indoor children's playground.

No 3 Rd at Alderbridge Way, Richmond. Tel: (604) 270 1344. Open: Mon–Tue & Sat 9am–5.30pm, Wed–Fri 9.30am–9pm, Sun noon–5pm.

Metrotown Centre

Greater Vancouver's largest shopping complex, just 15 minutes from downtown, with over 500 stores. All the big names and plenty of independents are represented here, and there are special events to entertain shoppers. The centre has different attractions: **Playdium** (*tel: (604) 434 6522; www.playdium.com*) is full of games and virtual reality. At **Metropolis**, start by dropping in at the customer service kiosk at the mall to pick up a discount card. Metropolis includes the largest food court in western Canada, meaning you'll have plenty of variety to choose from when you've worked up an appetite shopping. Station Square has the **Holiday Inn** (*tel: (604) 438 1881*) and cinemas (*tel: (604) 433 8438*).

4800 Kingsway, Burnaby. Open: Mon–Fri 10am–9pm, Sat 9.30am–6pm, Sun 11am–5.30pm.

Oakridge Centre

Over 150 quality stores here enjoy a bright and airy environment, with 20m (66ft) high vaulted skylights. There is also a cineplex.

41st Ave at Cambie St. Tel: (604) 261 2511. Open: Mon–Sat 9.30am–6pm (Wed–Fri 9pm), Sun noon–5pm.

Pacific Centre Mall

This mall spreads over and under three downtown city blocks, where

The Pacific Centre Mall

Light and bright Oakridge Centre

a three-storey waterfall, a glass rotunda and a skylit atrium attempt to bring the outdoors indoors. The redeveloped shopping centre features the Holt Renfrew Department Store, Canadian retailer Roots and about 160 other stores.
At Georgia and Howe sts. Tel: (604) 688 7236. Open: Mon–Sat 9.30am–7pm (Thur & Fri 9pm, Sat 6pm), Sun noon–6pm.

Park Royal Mall

This mall opened more than 40 years ago, when it was Canada's first major shopping centre. It has over 200 stores, half of which are independent traders. Other attractions include cinemas, bowling lanes and a golf driving range.
At the foot of the Lions Gate Bridge in West Vancouver. Tel: (604) 922 3211.

Open: Mon–Sat 10am–6pm (Thur & Fri 9pm); Sun noon–6pm.

Richmond Centre

All the usual department stores and international chains are gathered in this large mall near the airport.
No 3 Rd & Westminster Highway. Infoline tel: (604) 713 7467. Open: Mon–Sat 9.30am–6pm (Wed–Fri until 9pm), Sun 11am–6pm.

Sinclair Centre

This restored historic building houses a small cluster of exclusive shops circling an elegant skylit atrium, where musicians entertain and artists display their works.
757 West Hastings St. www.sinclaircentre.com. Open: Mon–Sat 10am–5.30pm.

Entertainment

Few people come to Vancouver for entertainment, except for the outdoor variety so bountifully offered by Mother Nature. But Vancouver is a quietly vibrant city and does offer such various indoor options as ballet, opera, classical music, rock, jazz, theatre and cinema, featuring respectable local, national and international talent.

The daily newspapers, *The Vancouver Sun* (*www.canada.com/vancouversun*) and *The Province* (*www.canada.com/theprovince*), along with the free weeklies, *The West Ender* and *Georgia Strait*, contain advertising and editorial reviews of current entertainment. *WHERE Vancouver* (*www.wherevancouver.com*), a compact monthly magazine free in most hotels, provides details of musical and theatrical performances, along with listings of cabarets, clubs and jazz gigs.

The **Arts Hotline** (*tel: (604) 684 2787; www.allianceforarts.com*) provides information on the performing arts, and the **Coastal Jazz and Blues Society** (*tel: (604) 872 5200; www.coastaljazz.ca*) offers information on the jazz scene.

For recorded information on current movies and cinema locations, call **Cineplex Odeon** (*tel: (604) 684 4000*), **Famous Players** (*tel: (604) 669 6000*), or the individual independent cinemas.

All kinds of street entertainers are scattered throughout the city, but especially on Robson Street. However, the best shows usually materialise on Granville Island on sunny Sunday afternoons. Here, on the wooden deck in front of the market overlooking False Creek, jugglers, clowns, storytellers, mime artists and musicians vie for attention. More formal outdoor concerts are held on Grouse Mountain and at Dr Sun Yat-Sen Garden on Carrall Street (*tel: (604) 689 7133*).

Tickets

Ticketmaster (*tel: (604) 280 4444; www.ticketmaster.ca*), which has outlets in Eaton's department store at downtown Pacific Centre and at information counters in major malls throughout the city, sells tickets for cultural and sporting events. Ticketmaster has special lines for arts events (*tel: (604) 280 3311*) and spectator sports (*tel: (604) 280 4400*).

For half-price day-of-show tickets, call Tickets Tonight at *(604) 684 2787*.

Ballet, opera and classical music

Ballet BC (*tel: (604) 732 5003*), **Canada's Royal Winnipeg Ballet** and such well-known visiting dance companies as the Kiev Ballet perform at the 2,800-seat Queen Elizabeth Theatre, at 630 Hamilton Street.

Also at the Queen Elizabeth, the **Vancouver Opera** (*tel: (604) 682 2871*) and visiting opera companies present contemporary productions and such timeless masterpieces as *The Marriage of Figaro* and *Don Pasquale.* At the adjacent **Playhouse Theatre Company** (*tel: (604) 873 3311*), the **Vancouver East Cultural Centre** (*tel: (604) 251 1363*), or, as it's affectionately known to locals, 'the Cultch', has an impressive programme of avant-garde theatre, international music, festivals and other arts events.

Many musical events are also held at the gracious and elegant **Orpheum**, located at 884 Granville, Smithe at Seymour (*tel: (604) 665 3035*). The Orpheum is the home of the **Vancouver Symphony Orchestra** (*Infoline: (604) 876 3434*), which also performs at various other Lower Mainland venues and at several outdoor locations during the summer.

Several classical chamber music groups run by professional musicians present complimentary concerts at a number of public sites. Free lunchtime concerts are often held on the plaza in Robson Square and in shopping malls around the city during July and August.

Headphones for people with hearing impairment are available at the Queen Elizabeth Theatre, the Vancouver Playhouse and the Orpheum. All these places are wheelchair-accessible. *For more information on Vancouver theatres, call (604) 665 3050, or visit www.city.vancouver.bc.ca/theatres*

Vancouver International Film Centre

Jazz

There are many good jazz artists and good places to enjoy them in Vancouver (*www.vancouverjazz.com*). Evenings offer a good choice, including the **Arts Club Backstage Lounge** at 1585 Johnston Street (*tel: (604) 687 1354*). The **Cellar Restaurant Jazz Club**, on 3611 W Broadway (*tel: (604) 738 1959*), features blues and cool jazz with name players and new talent. **Café Deux Soleils**, 2096 Commercial Drive (*tel: (604) 254 1195*), is the home of live entertainment, the schedule of which is subject to frequent change. The annual **Vancouver International Jazz Festival** is held throughout Vancouver in late June. For more information, call the **Jazz Hotline** (*tel: (604) 872 5200*) or visit *www.coastaljazz.ca*

Rock and contemporary music

Big Canadian and international names entertain regularly at **BC Place Stadium** (*tel: (604) 661 7242*) which seats 60,000 people; **Thunderbird Stadium** at 6081 Thunderbird Boulevard at the UBC campus (*tel: (604) 822 6121*), the **Pacific Coliseum** (*tel: (604) 253 2311*) by the Pacific National Exhibition grounds, and **GM Place** (*tel: (604) 899 7889*) – also known as The Garage, and home to Canuck's NHL Hockey Team for Vancouver.

Smaller places to hear good rock and local talent include the **Railway Club**, at 519 Dunsmuir (*tel: (604) 681 1625*), and **Richards** at 1036 Richards Street (*tel: (604) 687 6794*).

Check out *www.LiveMusic Vancouver.com* for up-to-date listings.

Theatre

The **Arts Club Theatre** (*tel: (604) 687 5315; www.artsclub.com*) offers the best in live theatre, ranging from classical Shakespeare to popular drama and contemporary works created by local playwrights. Programmes are presented year-round at the Mainstage and Revue theatres on Granville Island. Also on Granville Island, the **Waterfront Theatre** (*tel: (604) 687 3005*) stages outstanding Canadian plays, while the adjacent **Carousel Theatre** (*tel: (604) 685 6217*) entertains youngsters. The **Playhouse Theatre Company** (*tel: (604) 873 3311*), housed in the same building as the **Queen Elizabeth Theatre** at 630 Hamilton Street downtown, stages six full-scale productions each season, including classic and contemporary drama, comedy, musicals and at least one Canadian play. **Theatre Under The Stars** (*tel: (604) 687 0174*) has been putting on Broadway-style musicals for half a century at the Malkin Bowl bandstand outdoors in Stanley Park. The show continues from mid-July to mid-August, weather permitting. It is especially fun with a picnic under a full moon. The **Vancouver East Cultural Centre**, at 1895 Venables Street (*tel: (604) 251 1363; www.vecc.bc.ca*), seems to specialise in avant-garde theatre, complemented by visual art exhibitions.

The **TheatreSports League** (call for times, or see *www.vtsl.com*) presents hilarious improvisations, often involving the audience, at the **Arts Club Revue Stage**, 1585 Johnston Street (*tel: (604) 738 7013*), from Wednesday to Saturday at 8pm. At the **Lafflines Comedy Club**, 26 4th Street, New Westminster (*tel: (604) 525 2262*), stand-up comics from all over the continent entertain from Tuesday to Saturday at 9pm. **Yuk Yuk's**, in the Century Plaza Hotel, 1015 Burrard Street (*tel: (604) 696 9857*), also specialises in stand-up comedy.

The **Centre in Vancouver for Performing Arts**, at 777 Homer Street (*tel: (604) 602 0616*), features a variety of live performances, from musicals to solo performers, to ballet. Check *www.centreinvancouver.com* for the calendar.

Every September, **Vancouver International Fringe Festival** (*tel: (604) 257 0350*) has over 500 different performances – from Shakespeare to avant garde – in dozens of different venues.

Bard on the Beach

The **Bard on the Beach Theatre Society** (*tel: (604) 739 0559*) presents Shakespearean favourites in an open-ended candy-striped tent seating 300 people in Vanier Park adjacent to the Planetarium, on evenings in July and August. The setting is spectacular, as

Open-air performances are always a big draw

the stage has a backdrop of the North Shore mountains and sky coloured by the setting sun. Prices are reasonable, and reservations are recommended.

Cinema

Vancouver has dozens of cinemas showing the latest feature films. Most are to be found downtown on the Granville Street Mall. The Park Royal Mall in West Vancouver has a multiplex; Metrotown Centre at Burnaby has two; and there are also several small cinemas in the Royal Centre Mall under the Hyatt Regency Hotel.

The **Pacific Cinématèque**, at 1131 Howe Street (*24-hour hotline: (604) 688 FILM*), is a non-profit, educational society dedicated to the enjoyment and study of film. Emphasis is on independent, non-mainstream films and classics.

Esplanade 6 Cinemas is at 200 West Esplanade, North Vancouver (*tel: (604) 983 2762*). **Station Square 7 Cinemas** is at Metrotown Centre, Burnaby (*tel: (604) 434 7711*).

The Ridge, at 3131 Arbutus Street (*tel: (604) 738 6311*), also features the classical and offbeat, serves delicious carrot cake and cappuccino, and has a kiddies' room.

Movie theatre giant Cineplex runs several movie complexes in Vancouver and the surrounding neighbourhoods. There's **Station Square** at Metrotown Centre in Burnaby (*tel: (604) 434 7711*) and **Richmond Centre 6** at the

Richmond Shopping Centre (*tel: (604) 273 7173*). The **Scotia Bank Theatre Vancouver** is downtown at 900 Burrard Street (*tel: (604) 630 1407*). The **Cineplex Odeon** is in North Vancouver at 333 Brooksbank Avenue (*tel: (604) 985 4215*). **Cinemark Tinseltown** is also downtown at 88 West Pender (*tel: (604) 806 0799*).

For those seeking the biggest of the big screen, there's an **IMAX Theatre** at Canada Place (*tel: (604) 682 IMAX*) and the **Alcan OMNIMAX** at Science World (*tel: (604) 443 7443*).

The annual **Vancouver International Film Festival** (*tel: (604) 685 8297; www.viff.org*), which takes place in early October, offers the best in current cinema from around the world.

Casinos

Gambling is highly regulated in Canada. Two of the major casinos, the **Great Canadian Casino** (*tel: (604) 303 1000; open: daily 10am–6am*) and the brand new **Gateway Casino** (*tel: (604) 523 3550*), abide by this. Dice are not permitted, so games are limited to roulette and blackjack. Non-alcoholic beverages and snacks are available. Fifty per cent of the proceeds go to local charities. The Great Canadian Casino has four locations in the Lower Mainland. The closest one to downtown is in the Holiday Inn at 709 West Broadway. The Gateway Casino has 800 slot machines, a poker room, gaming tables and more. There's also live entertainment, a sports bar and a Chinese restaurant. The casino complex – the largest in British Columbia – is at Westminster Highway between Boundary Road and Gifford Street.

Discos and clubs
Bacchus
The bar/lounge in the Wedgewood Hotel is the place to go if you want to rub shoulders with celebs in town for Vancouver's hot film production scene.
845 Hornby St. Tel: (604) 689 7777.
Crush Champagne Lounge
See and be seen at this Miami-style hot spot. Extensive champagne selection, plus a full bar.
1180 Granville St. Tel: (604) 684 0355.
Ginger Sixty-Two
A posh Fellini-esque ambience with a multitude of music styles.
1219 Granville St. Tel: (604) 688 5494.
Richards on Richards
Show up early to beat the lines, then stay to dance all night. Popular with the hip dance floor crowd, the club has an upstairs bar and balcony for checking out the scene.
1036 Richards St. Tel: (604) 687 6794.
Shine
A trendy club that looks like *Clockwork Orange,* all white and glossy.
364 Water St, Gastown.
Tel: (604) 408 4321.
Sonar
State-of-the-art techno club for the rave crowd, in the heart of historic Gastown.
66 Water St. Tel: (604) 683 6695.

The Cellar Nightclub
Live house bands – BritRock and top-yo & hip hop.
1006 Granville St.
Tel: (604) 605 4350.
The Yale
Once voted the No 1 bar in town, it offers live music every day.
1300 Granville St. Tel: (604) 681 9253.
Vanilla Room
High above Langley in high style. Faux fur and leather décor, 'virtual art tables' and VIP service.
6001 196A St, Langley.
Tel: (604) 530 2026.
Voda
Attracts crowds of all ages to an intriguing interior of 1950s modernism. Waterfalls, rocks and hundreds of candles are a backdrop for Latin, R&B, funk and reggae.
In the Weston Grand Hotel, 783 Homer St. Tel: (604) 684 3003.

Dinner plus
Blarney Stone
This lively Gastown restaurant features Irish and contemporary entertainment, starting at 7pm.
216 Carrall St. Tel: (604) 687 4322.
Shark Club Bar & Grill
This sports bar provides a warm ambience, created by a fireplace and rich mahogany surroundings. Sports fans enjoy the sports memorabilia, pool tables, dartboards and 30 television sets.
180 West Georgia St.
Tel: (604) 687 4275.

Children

Vancouver offers an abundance of attractions to entertain and educate youngsters. Some activities mentioned here are described in more detail in other parts of this book. For more suggestions, check Victoria Bushnell's Kids Vancouver *or Fodor's* Vancouver with Kids, *and the Friday 'Family Fun' column in* The Vancouver Sun, *or try www.findfamilyfun.com*

Downtown

CN IMAX Theatre
A 400-seat cinema with a five-storey high wrap-around screen.
Canada Place. Tel: (604) 682 IMAX; www.imax.com/vancouver

H R MacMillan Space Centre
Take a virtual voyage through space, have breakfast with an astronaut and learn about what it's like to live in space. The Space Centre also has a planetarium.
1100 Chestnut St. Tel: (604) 738 7827; www.hrmacmillanspacecentre.com

Science World
Provides enough hands-on educational enjoyment for a whole day. The OMNIMAX cinema presents six shows daily. (*See pp68–9.*)
1455 Quebec St. Tel: (604) 443 7440; www.scienceworld.bc.ca

Stanley Park is a wonderful playground and children especially love the Miniature Railway (*tel: (604) 257 8531; www.city.vancouver.bc.ca/parks/parks/ stanley; open: 11am–4pm daily*), and the squirrels and raccoons which hang around Lost Lagoon. There are tours on an old-fashioned horse-drawn wagon through the park (*tel: (604) 681 5115*). (*See pp70–73.*)

Aquarium
Kids enjoy touching the sea cucumbers, anemones, starfish and chitons (molluscs), and also love watching sea otters in a playful mood as they socialise underwater. (*See pp72–3.*)
Tel: (604) 685 3364; 24-hour info: (604) 659 FISH; www.vanaqua.org

For more water fun, there is the saltwater swimming pool – an enjoyable and safe option, which is supervised by lifeguards at Second Beach (*tel: (604) 257 8370*); and then there are the water parks on the Seawall near Lumberman's Arch and beside the fire engine playground near Pacific Avenue. Kids can burn up extra energy by cycling around the scenic 10km (6-mile) Seawall.

Bicycle rentals are available near the Georgia Street entrance to the park.

Granville Island

SeaBus

Start by taking the SeaBus from downtown to Granville – the views from the water are spectacular. Get a day pass and take the SeaBus everywhere!
Start at the SeaBus Terminal at Canada Place.

Kids Only Market

Houses two dozen shops and other diversions. Special events are organised for weekends. On the south side is a Play Centre for three- to five-year-olds.
1496 Cartwright St. Tel: (604) 689 8447. Open: daily 9am–6pm.

Weary parents can revive themselves with a cappuccino at The Cat's Meow, while children shower each other with big fire hoses attached to revolving fire hydrants at the supervised **Water Park** in front.

Arts Umbrella

Two-week, day and half-day camps in summer are run for kids up to the age of 18. Classes include sculpture, dance, drama, painting, drawing and wood-carving. Reservations are advised.
1286 Cartwright St. Tel: (604) 681 5268; www.artsumbrella.com. 9am–3.30pm (shorter for pre-school children).

Families can share outdoor fun with rental kayaks from Ecomarine, at 1668 Duranleau Street (*tel: (604) 689 7575*).

University of British Columbia

The **Museum of Anthropology** (*tel: (604) 822 5087; www.moa.ubc.ca*) lets children beat hanging drums and pull out dozens of drawers to examine native Indian toys, jewellery and clothing. Children enjoy feeding the fish at the Nitobe Japanese Gardens.

East Vancouver and Burnaby

Playland at the PNE (Pacific National Exhibition) Grounds

The rides are open from April to October. Attractions include the roller coaster, log-chute rides and the new 'Breakdance' and 'Gladiator' rides. Watching chickens hatch and cows calve during the Pacific National Exhibition in the last two weeks of August are especially interesting.
Tel: (604) 253 2311; www.pne.ca

Burnaby's Heritage Village and Carousel (*tel: (604) 293 6501; www.burnaby.ca*) is an open-air museum with costumed guides and old buildings recreating life between the 1890s and 1920s. **The Carousel** has 36 wooden horses, a chariot and four metal ponies.

North Vancouver

Maplewood Farm (*tel: (604) 929 5610; www.maplewoodfarm.bc.ca*) is a 2-hectare (5-acre) park where children can get acquainted with farm animals, have a pony ride and watch milking.

Capilano Suspension Bridge and Treetops – safe but scary, the suspension bridge hangs 70m (230ft) above a river and leads to a trail through unspoilt rainforest. Treetops Adventure offers a squirrel's-eye view.
Tel: (604) 985 7474.

Sport and leisure

Vancouver is an absolute mecca for sports lovers. The long days of summer are great for golf and tennis; the beaches and sea breezes appeal to swimmers and sailors; there are lots of trails for cyclists and hikers; and local fresh and salt waters teem with life for eager anglers and divers. Come June, Vancouver hosts the Alcan Dragon Boat Festival, North America's longest-running event of its kind (www.adbf.com), and in winter skiers head for the mountains.

LAND SPORTS

Bowling

Vancouver has 20 bowling alleys, some five-pin, some ten-pin. Check the *Yellow Pages* for details of opening times.

Bungee and ropes courses

Navigate the treetops or plunge head first off a bridge at Wild Play, an adventure park just outside Nanaimo. Kids aged 12 and over are welcome.
*35 Nanaimo River Rd.
Tel: (250) 716 7874.*

Caving

There are about 2,000 caves in BC, mostly on Vancouver Island, all in original condition, with no walkways. Only 600 of them have been charted.

Popular caves for exploring include the Black Hole (situated in virgin rainforest), the Horne Lake Caves, Paradise Lost and the Artlish River Cave. Cody Caves offers one- and three-hour seasonal tours – including safety gear – at Cody Caves Provincial Park (*tel: (250) 353 7364*).

Cycling

The Stanley Park Seawall (*see pp74–5*) provides the perfect path for an hour of urban cycling. The paved trail following the SkyTrain route from Main St station to New Westminster is also relatively flat and passes 32 parks and playgrounds. Spokes Bicycle Rentals (*tel: (604) 688 5141*) and other downtown operations rent bicycles by the hour or by the day.

Golfing

The province's 160 golf courses include 17 in Vancouver, all open to the public. A letter of introduction from your home club provides entry to private courses. Several par-three courses are scattered throughout the city. Langara Golf Course at 6706 Alberta Street (*tel: (604) 713 1816*) is one of the best in BC; another is the McCleery Golf

Course in South Vancouver at 7188 MacDonald Street (*tel: (604) 251 8181*).

Hiking and walking

Most major parks in and around Vancouver have well-marked circuits for scenic wilderness hikes and walks. The Stanley Park Seawall is the best walk close to downtown (*see pp74–5*). Lynn Canyon is an equally spectacular, but a cheaper and quieter, alternative to Capilano (and it has its own suspension bridge). Lynn Canyon Ecology Centre on the North Shore (*tel: (604) 981 3103*) provides films and summer nature programmes about the environment.

Horse riding

Urban equestrians enjoy the trails at Langley 204 Stables at 543 204th Street (*tel: (604) 533 7978*), which offers 18km (11 miles) of trails on good-quality horses. Riders with more time may want to rough it with wranglers on the range, such as the one at Ashcroft known as the Sundance Guest Ranch (*tel: (250) 453 2422 or freephone (800) 553 3533; www.sundanceguestranch.com*).

Paragliding

'Flight-seeing' is an exhilarating way to view the spectacular BC scenery for those who have the nerve. Mount Seven in the Rockies is a site of international competitions for paragliding and hang-gliding, but for a beginner's introduction to the sport Grouse Mountain is ideal. Flights in tandem with a professional pilot are available daily between March and September (weather permitting). Call First Flight Paragliding (*tel: (604) 980 9311; www.grousemountain.com*).

Rock climbing

In a region with so many mountains, rock climbing is almost an instinct. Learners practise in Lighthouse Park in West Vancouver on cliffs overhanging the water, and then move on to tough mountain challenges. **Cliffhanger Indoor Rock Climbing Centre** (*tel: (604) 874 2400*) has nearly 1,000sq m (10,760sq ft) of walls to climb. **Playland** (*tel: (604) 253 2311*) offers a 12m (39ft) outdoor climbing wall in the Extreme Action Zone of the grounds. Contact the Federation of Mountain Clubs of BC (*tel: (604) 873 6096; www.mountainclubs.bc.ca*).

Skiing

Vancouver's North Shore has three ski areas within a half-hour drive of the city centre. The nearest is Grouse Mountain (1,250m/4,101ft), where in good weather skiers enjoy spectacular views down to the city centre and across Georgia Strait to the Gulf Islands and Vancouver Island.

Cypress Bowl to the west and Mount Seymour to the east also offer nordic skiing. Cypress and Grouse are lit for evening skiing until 10pm. All three mountains have equipment rentals and restaurants. For more information, visit *www.skihills.com*

Skiing

BC is one of Canada's top ski playgrounds. The combination of the moderate climate with the proximity of Vancouver airport to good ski facilities, comfortable accommodation and challenging terrain appeals to skiers from around the globe.

When moist, cold air from the Pacific meets the coastal mountains, the result is big flakes of snow which pack the mountain peaks and slopes.

The three North Shore mountains, Cypress, Grouse and Seymour – all within a half-hour drive from Vancouver city centre – offer spectacular sea and city vistas, along with good ski facilities open day and evening from November to April when the snows permit.

Japanese skiers have named Whistler/Blackcomb, fast becoming a subject for superlatives all over the world, their favourite ski area, leaving Vail, Chamonix and Zermatt in the shadows. Here, a two-hour drive north from Vancouver, high-speed quad chairs and other lifts run up spectacular slopes to a variety of gentle runs for novices, alpine chutes, glades, groomed runs, moguls and vast areas of backcountry for skilled skiers.

Hemlock, in the Fraser Valley, also accommodates overnight guests at its cosy alpine village, and offers 30km (19 miles) of groomed trails. Manning Park Resort is a small, family-style ski area at the northern end of the Cascades.

Nordic skiing along trails in the Lower Mainland presents a range of exciting challenges. The 16km (10 miles) of hilly tracks and packed trails at Hollyburn Ridge on Cypress Mountain are open all day and evening until 10pm. The Diamond Head area in Garibaldi Park has high glaciers, with an overnight hut available at Elfin Lakes. The Hemlock

SOME POPULAR SKI RESORTS

Vancouver
Cypress Mountain Ski Area. *Tel: (604) 419 SNOW; www.cypressmountain.com*
Grouse Mountain. *Tel: (604) 980 9311 or (604) 986 6262; www.grousemountain.com*
Mount Seymour Ski Resort. *Tel: (604) 986 2261; www.mountseymour.com*

British Columbia
Whistler/Blackcomb, Whistler. *Tel: (604) 932 3434; www.whistler-blackcomb.com*
Silver Star Mountain Ski Resort, Vernon. *Tel: (250) 542 0224; www.skisilverstar.com*
Big White Ski Resort, Kelowna. *Tel: (250) 765 3101; www.bigwhite.com*

Valley loop comprises 30km (19 miles) of groomed trails, good for both cross-country and telemark skiing.

Other downhill and nordic ski areas are scattered throughout the BC interior. For the adventurous, there is heli-skiing in the Bugaboos and at Tyax, north of Whistler, and there is snowcat skiing in the Selkirk Mountains.

There are lots of ski options in BC

Tennis

More than 200 public courts, scattered throughout the city, are free and operate on a first come, first served basis. Stanley Park charges a court fee in summer.

WATER SPORTS

Vancouver has water on three sides, and BC has more than 7,000km (4,350 miles) of coastline, 11,000 rivers and creeks, 6,000 lakes, 30 coastal marine parks and countless tidal inlets, offering unmatched opportunities for adventure. (*See* Getting Away, *pp127–31*.)

Canoeing

A number of companies specialise in outdoor adventures. They can arrange canoeing trips for half a day or week-long excursions with full catering. Lotus Land Tours (*tel: (604) 684 4922 or freephone (800) 528 3531; www.lotuslandtours.com*) offer a half-day nature adventure with free pick-up in Vancouver.

Fishing

A fishing licence (saltwater or freshwater, or both), sold in major downtown department stores and in sporting goods shops, is essential. The interior season extends from May to October, while coastal waters may operate year-round. Numerous rivers and lakes contain trout and salmon. Arctic grayling, pike and walleye inhabit northern waters, while the boundary areas contain smallmouth bass and yellow perch. Sturgeon live in the Fraser and Columbia rivers and bass are found on Vancouver Island.

Spring or chinook salmon and coho are the most popular saltwater catches, although some anglers prefer the challenges of sockeye, pink and chum salmon. Coastal waters also harbour halibut, flounder, sole, red snapper, perch, greenling, ling cod and the spotted sea-run cut-throat trout. Such shellfish as abalone, clams, oysters, crabs, mussels, scallops, shrimps and prawns also inhabit these waters. Restrictions concerning size and species are outlined in the *BC Tidal Waters Sport Fishing Guide.*

You can either take a fishing charter, which will look after everything, or you can rent a motorboat. Sooke Fishing Charters offers B&B and fishing charter combination packages out of south Vancouver Island (*tel: (888) 430 7456*). Sewell's Marina has both bareboat rentals and charter options.

Watch the expert boat racers skim over the waters

A killer whale at close quarters

Kayaking

Ecomarine at 1668 Duranleau St (*tel: (604) 689 7575; www.ecomarine.com*), on Granville Island, rents kayaks all year round.

A two-hour rental allows ample time to glide along the quiet waters of False Creek past the market deck, the floating houseboat homes, Science World and the residential community along the south shore. Both one- and two-seater kayaks are available. Talaysay Tours has kayaking, canoeing, hiking and snowshoeing tours led by Candace Campo, a First Nations guide with a rich knowledge of local flora and fauna and native legends (*tel: (604) 628 8555, freephone (800) 605 4643; www.talaysaytours.com*).

Batstar Adventure Tours have well-organised, relaxed, fun kayaking tours into the wilderness of Vancouver Island's Broken Islands group using top-of-the-line equipment, luxury tents and serving gourmet food (*tel: freephone (877) 449 1230; www.batstar.com*).

Motor boating

Canada's largest fleet of self-drive rental boats is moored in Horseshoe Bay, 17km (10 1/2 miles) northwest of downtown. Here, Sewell's Marina (*tel: (604) 921 3474; www.sewellsmarina.com*) rents boats by the hour and longer – a great way to explore the coastline and nearby islands.

River rafting

In this exhilarating social sport, a dozen or so novices and a couple of expert guides challenge the white water. Such Vancouver companies as Hyak Wilderness Adventures (*tel: (604) 734 8622, freephone (800) 663 7238; www.hyak.com*) offer trips varying from a heart-thumping afternoon ride to six-day trips through the stunning scenery of BC's most exciting rivers.

Scuba diving

BC's underwater world is a submarine jungle of graceful giant anemones, towering sea-whips, gorgonian corals and other marine life.

Howe Sound is one of the most popular diving areas, and at Porteau Cove, on its eastern shore, a Provincial Marine Park has been established, with old ship hulls forming an artificial reef.

Though the surface waters are reasonably warm, the temperature below the thermocline persists at about 10°C (50°F), so divers will need a 6mm (¼in) neoprene wet suit or, even better, a custom dry suit.

Equipment is available for hire from a number of dive shops, including BC Dive and Kayak Adventures, at 1695

West 4th Avenue (*tel: (604) 732 1344; www.bcdive.com*). The International Diving Centre at 2572 Arbutus Street (*tel: (604) 736 2541; www.diveidc.com*) organises day, weekend or longer trips.

Swimming

English Bay beaches offer good swimming in summer, but seekers of solitude may prefer Savary Island and Desolation Sound further north, where the waters are just as warm.

The freshwater pool at Second Beach in Stanley Park and Kits pool (Vancouver's only saltwater pool) at 2305 Cornwall (*tel: (604) 731 0011*) are open from May to September.

Indoor pools at the University of British Columbia (UBC) Aquatic Centre at 6121 University Boulevard (*tel: (604) 822 4522*), the Vancouver Aquatic Centre at 1050 Beach Avenue (*tel: (604) 665 3424*) and the YMCA at 955 Burrard downtown (*tel: (604) 689 YMCA; www.vanymca.ca*) are open day and evening throughout the year. Check out *www.vancouverparks.ca* for a complete list of city beaches and pools.

SPECTATOR SPORTS
Whale watching

Watching these great mammals of the Pacific is a favourite spectator sport of both residents and visitors. Johnstone Strait, between Vancouver Island and the mainland, is home to the world's largest concentration of killer whales that can be seen on a daily basis.

These sheltered waters, about 400km (249 miles) northwest of Vancouver, are home to 12 pods, totalling approximately 135 killer whales. When conditions permit, you can listen with a hydrophone to orcas emitting their famous songs and clicks. The total killer whale population of BC is around 300. The whales have a low birthrate and a low mortality rate. The males may live for up to 50 years, while the females

Whale watching is a popular excursion

The Vancouver Canucks take on the Phoenix Coyotes

may live twice as long. Johnstone Strait is also home for many sea birds and bald eagles, salmon, seals, sea lions, porpoises, minke whales, humpback whales, harbour seals and Pacific white-sided dolphins.

Off the west coast of Vancouver Island, spring is the time to see the big grey whales migrating from Baja California to Alaska. Several companies, such as **Orca Spirit Adventures** (*tel: 1 (888) 672 ORCA*), provide watching tours. Bring binoculars. **Vancouver Whale Watch** in Richmond is the only whale-watching outfit on the lower mainland (*tel: (604) 274 9565; www.vancouverwhalewatch.com*).

Team sports

For those who enjoy the roar of the crowd, there are the BC Lions (*tel: (604) 589 ROAR*) who play home games in the Canadian Football League at BC Place Stadium (777 Pacific Boulevard); the Vancouver Canadians AAA baseball team – one step below

major league standard – (*tel: (604) 872 5232; www.canadiansbaseball.com*), who perform at Nat Bailey Stadium (4601 Ontario St at 30th Ave); the Vancouver Whitecaps soccer team (*tel: (604) 669 9283 WAVE; Swangard Stadium, in Burnaby*); and, in winter, the Vancouver Canucks ice hockey team who compete in the National Hockey League at GM Place downtown. Information on seasons, game times, venues and tickets is available from the Travel InfoCentre (*tel: (604) 683 2000*).

Horse racing

Horse racing takes place from mid-April to the end of November at Vancouver's Hastings Racecourse (*tel: (604) 254 1631, freephone (800) 677 7702; www.hastingspark.com*). Betting diners can watch the races on closed-circuit television, but the view of Mount Seymour across Burrard Inlet from the stands is so spectacular that it would be a shame to miss it.

Food and drink

East and West meet in Vancouver in an amazing variety of restaurants, some Oriental, some European, some African, some North American, and others which artfully combine and innovate to create new cuisines.

Fine foods and wines are often found in Vancouver at lower prices than in Europe. Dinner usually costs more than lunch for the same menu, and breakfast is the bargain of the day. Many restaurants are closed on Monday. Except for fast-food places, reservations are recommended for lunch during the week and for dinner on Friday and Saturday evenings. Most restaurants accept major credit cards. Restaurants do not add a service charge, so a tip of between 10 and 20 per cent is welcome.

Restaurants listed are categorised according to price per person for a full-course meal, not including alcohol.

★	under C$10
★★	C$10–20
★★★	C$20–35
★★★★	over C$35

Breakfast and brunch

Elbow Room Cafe ★★
Plastered with clippings and photos of the rich and famous, and vibrates with the energy of the two owners.
560 Davie St. Tel: (604) 685 3628.

James Street Café ★★
Big pancakes and a variety of eggs Benedict.
4441 Boundary Road, Burnaby. Tel: (604) 430 2223.

Joe's Grill ★★★
Highly recommended for its delicious breakfasts.
2061 West 4th Ave in Kitsilano. Tel: (604) 736 6588.

Lucky Diner ★★
French coffee in a renovated Yaletown warehouse.
1269 Hamilton St. Tel: (604) 662 8048.

Sophie's Cosmic Cafe ★
A great place to take kids for breakfast or otherwise.
2095 W Fourth Ave. Tel: (604) 732 6810.

Sunshine Diner ★★
Top-notch food (especially breakfast, eggs and waffles), fast service.
2756 W Broadway. Tel: (604) 733 7717.

Chinese restaurants

Floata Seafood Restaurant ★★★
The biggest Chinese banquet restaurant in the heart of Vancouver's Chinatown.

400–180 Keefer St.
Tel: (604) 602 0368.

Hon's Wun-Tun House ★★

A popular place for Cantonese cuisine.
1339 Robson St.
Tel: (604) 685 0871.

The Pink Pearl ★★★

The city's best Cantonese restaurant.
1132 East Hastings St.
Tel: (604) 253 4316.

Shanghai Xin Hua Lou ★★

Best dumplings in town and northern-style *dim sum.*
4136 Main St. Tel: (604) 879 5818.

Shao Lin Noodle Restaurant ★

Inexpensive but yummy noodle dishes in a busy atmosphere.
548 W Broadway.
Tel: (604) 873 1816.

Sun Sui Wah ★★

Good *dim sum* and congee, and very popular.
3888 Main St.
Tel: (604) 872 8822.

Szechuan Chongqing Seafood Restaurant ★★

Spicy Szechuan-style food, lunch specials.
1668 W Broadway.
Tel: (604) 734 1668.

Wing Wah Shanghai Szechuan ★★

260 E Broadway.

Japanese restaurants

Hapa Izakaya ★★

You'll spot this popular noodle place by the queue outside the door.
1479 Robson St.
Tel: (604) 689 4272.

Raku ★★★★

Tasty and unusual Japanese dishes.
4422 W 10th.
Tel: (604) 222 8188.

Shiru-Bay Chopstick Café ★★★

Stylish Tokyo style bistro.
1193 Hamilton. Tel: (604) 408 9315.

Sui Sha Ya ★★

Fusion Japanese and all-you-can-eat sushi.
101–1401 W Broadway.
Tel: (604) 733 8886.

Tanpopo ★★

One of Vancouver's first all-you-can-eat sushi spots and still serving great sashimi. Frenzied

A crêpe shop in laid-back Kitsilano

Dim sum brunch

A Sunday-morning crowd slowly moves up a staircase to the second floor, to a cultural experience and fast food at its finest. This is Ming's in Vancouver's Chinatown, one of the biggest and best *dim sum* restaurants in town.

A dish of small steamed or fried savoury dumplings containing various fillings, *dim sum* means 'a little bit of heart' in Cantonese, and both Cantonese and other Canadians are eating to their hearts' delight. It is a lively and happy occasion and often a family affair.

Dim sum regulars arrive early and sit near the kitchen for the first choice of freshest food. A procession of little carts, carrying stacks of steaming bamboo baskets and stainless steel containers filled with dozens of different delights, are wheeled among the tables, where hundreds of people are enjoying some of the more than 50 listed delicacies.

Typical *dim sum* dish

A *dim sum* breakfast spread

Popular *dim sum* includes *ha gow*, a thin rice dough wrapped around bits of prawns and bamboo shoots and steamed; *cha siu bao*, dumpling-like buns filled with barbecued pork; and sticky rice wrapped in lotus leaves.

Dim sum diners can eat a little, or a lot, and pay accordingly. Each portion usually contains two or three bite-sized pieces. The complimentary green jasmine tea, or the robust black *bo lei*, goes well with *dim sum*. When the teapot is empty, simply lift the lid and the waiter quickly refills it. To say thank you, tap your first two fingers on the table. Chinese and local beer go well with *dim sum*.

Dim sum restaurants are not renowned for décor. Arrive early and the place looks bleak. Arrive later, and the animated eaters, the ebony-eyed waitresses and the choreography of the carts in the moveable feast create a splendid scenario. And the noise is a joyful one.

atmosphere but sushi fanatics love it.

1122 Denman St.
Tel: (604) 681 7777.

Tojo Japanese Restaurant ★★★★

One of the best in North America.

1133 W Broadway.
Tel: (604) 872 8050.

Yoshi's on Denman ★★★

Rated by Vancouver Magazine as one of the city's best. Fresh seafood, great ambience and patio dining.

689 Denman St.
Tel: (604) 738 8226.

Enjoy a beer at Fogg n' Suds

Indian restaurants

Heaven and Earth ★★★

Authentic Indian cuisine, sitar music and a relaxed atmosphere.

1754 W 4th Ave.
Tel: (604) 732 5313.

Tandoori King ★★★

A favourite among the city's food specialists.

689 E 65th St.
Tel: (604) 327 8900.

Thai restaurants

Montri-Thai ★★

City restaurateurs like to dine here.

3629 W Broadway.
Tel: (604) 738 9888.

European Restaurants

Athene's ★★

Family run, generous portions, lively environment.

3618 W Broadway.
Tel: (604) 731 4135.

The Chef and Carpenter ★★★★

A top chef creates fine French food here.

1745 Robson St.
Tel: (604) 687 2700.

CinCin ★★★

Contemporary Italian, wood-fired grill, stunning desserts.

1154 Robson St.
Tel: (604) 688 7338.

Le Gavroche ★★★★

In the cosy and charming upstairs of an old house (the two window tables offer a great harbour view), Le Gavroche has received several awards for fine cuisine, which ranges from classic European dishes to *mahi mahi* and smoked duck.

1616 Alberni St.
Tel: (604) 685 3924.

Lumiere ★★★

French cuisine can be enjoyed inside or on the

patio in fine weather.
Valet parking is a bonus.
2551 W Broadway.
Tel: (604) 739 8185.

Omitsky Kosher Foods ★
Great Hebrew food,
from corned beef to
matzoh ball soup.
5866 Cambie St.
Tel: (604) 321 1818.

Villa del Lupo ★★★
Timeless Italian cuisine
in a Mediterranean-style
setting.
869 Hamilton St.
Tel: (604) 688 7436.

Fast food

A&W ★
A favourite with younger
children.
Sinclair Centre.
Tel: (604) 687 4186.

Babylon Café ★
Delicious chicken
shawarma, takeaway
only.
716 Robson St.
Tel: (604) 677 3522.

The Cactus Club ★★
Famous for Mexican
fajitas and burgers.
1136 Robson St.
Tel: (604) 687 3278.

Café Crêpe ★
Sweet or savoury crêpes,
made to order.
874 Granville St.
Tel: (604) 806 0845.

C-Lover's Fish & Chips ★
Tempura-like batter and
great chips.
1660 Pemberton Ave.
Tel: (604) 980 9993.

Flying Wedge Pizza ★★
You pay a bit more,
but great pizza.
Numerous outlets in
the city, but this one
is in Vancouver's
beautiful library.
207–345 Robson St.
Tel: (604) 689 7078.

**Fogg n' Suds
Restaurant ★**
Fun and casual,
with an international
menu.
1323 Robson St.
Tel: (604) 683 2337.

Food Fair ★
There is fast food
from many countries
in this mall food
area.
*Pacific Centre, Howe
and Dunsmuir.*

The Noodle Express ★★
Among the best of the
Japanese sushi and
noodle houses.
382 Robson St.
Tel: (604) 609 2688.

**The Old Spaghetti
Factory ★★**
Good family fare – a
great place to take
children.

53 Water St, Gastown.
Tel: (604) 684 1288.

Vera's Burger Shack ★
Award-winning burgers.
1030 Davie St.
Tel: (604) 893 8372.

Fish restaurants

C ★★★
Dubbed Vancouver's
most innovative and
creative seafood
restaurant – try the
octopus-wrapped
scallops or soft-shell
crab.
2–1600 Howe St.
Tel: (604) 681 1164.

**Cannery Seafood
House ★★★★**
Down on the docks
and elegantly rustic, the
views here vie with the
freshest fish.
2205 Commissioner St.
Tel: (604) 254 9606.

The Fish House ★★★★
Exceptional seafood
and fresh oyster bar,
with sunny patios
overlooking
English Bay.
8901 Stanley Park Drive.
Tel: (604) 681 7275.

Go Fish! ★★
Fresh local seafood on
Fisherman's Wharf.
1505 W 1st Ave.
Tel: (604) 730 5039.

Places to talk

**Bacchus Restaurant
& Lounge ★★★★**
The place in town for
mood lighting, quiet
conversation and a good
chance of spotting well-
known celebrities.
845 Hornby St.
Tel: (604) 689 7777.

**Hotel Vancouver
Lounge ★★**
One of the city's great
meeting places.
900 W Georgia St.
Tel: (604) 684 3131.

Indica ★★
Indian-inspired cuisine in
an intimate environment.
1795 Pendrell St.
Tel: (604) 609 3530.

Joe Fortes ★★★
Haunt of yuppies, and a
good place for people-
watching.
777 Thurlow St.
Tel: (604) 669 1940.

La Bodega ★★
Tasty *tapas* here include
the best fried chicken in
town, and patrons love
the informal Spanish
atmosphere.
1277 Howe St.
Tel: (604) 684 8814/5.

**Seawall Bar and
Bistro ★★★**
A cosy place in West
Coast nautical style

that is comfortable even
when packed.
Bayshore Hotel,
1601 W Georgia St.
Tel: (604) 682 3377.

**Pan Pacific Lobby
Lounge ★★★**
Spectacular views
of the Alaska cruise
ships and the harbour.
999 Canada Place.
Tel: (604) 662 8111.

Sylvia Hotel Bar ★★
The best place to
watch the sun set over
English Bay.
Beach and Gilford.
Tel: (604) 681 9321.

Zin ★★★
Patrons here enjoy great
food, live music and
wickered comfort, while
looking out on Robson
Street.
Pacific Palisades Hotel,
1277 Robson St.
Tel: (604) 408 1700.

Vegetarian food

Bodhi Vegetarian ★★★
Provides good, no-meat
meals.
3932 Fraser.
Tel: (604) 873 3848.

Dharma Kitchen ★
Completely vegan –
no animal products
of any kind. Specialises
in rice bowls.

3667 W Broadway.
Tel: (604) 738 3899.

**Greens and
Gourmet ★★★★**
Soft new-age music,
bright greenery-filled
rooms and fine
vegetarian cuisine.
2582 W Broadway.
Tel: (604) 737 7373.

Naam Restaurant ★★
A famous 24-hour
vegetarian restaurant
with a wood fireplace
and heated patio.
2724 W 4th Ave.
Tel: (604) 738 7151.

Planet Veg ★
Fast vegetarian near Kits
Beach; indoor and
outdoor seating.
1941 Cornwall Ave.
Tel: (604) 734 1001.

Rime ★★
Tasty vegetarian entrées
at this Turkish
restaurant. Live
entertainment.
1130 Commercial.
Tel: (604) 215 1130.

West Coast

Bishop's ★★★★
Consistently praised for its
impeccable service,
Bishop's also has an
extensive cellar with a good
range of Californian and
Pacific Northwest wines.

There are stunning views from the Pan Pacific

2183 W 4th Ave.
Tel: (604) 738 2025.
**Bud's Halibut and
Chips ★★**
Not surprisingly, the
halibut here is
particularly good.
1007 Denman St.
Tel: (604) 683 0661.
Café Madeleine ★★
No madeleines on the
menu, but the
sandwiches are excellent;
a favourite with
University of British
Columbia students.
3761 W 10th Ave.
Tel: (604) 224 5558.
Delilah's ★★★
The old railroad-style
menus here offer a set-

price, two-course and
five-course dinner.
1789 Comox St.
Tel: (604) 687 3424.
**Observatory
Restaurant ★★★★**
The magnificent views
from the summit, and
the inclusive Skyride
trip up the mountain, are
just two good reasons to
dine at the Observatory.
The superbly cooked
West Coast specialities
would be worth doing
the 'Grouse Grind'
hike for.
Grouse Mountain, 6400
Nancy Greene Way,
North Vancouver.
Tel: (604) 980 9311.

The Only Café ★★
The 'only' theme is
carried on beyond the
name of this restaurant –
it only serves fish, only
perfect, and is the only
restaurant in town
without a washroom!
20 E Hastings St.
Tel: (604) 681 6546.
Raincity Grill ★★★★
A 'buy local, eat seasonal'
restaurant. This is a gem.
Always makes 'best' lists.
1193 Denman St.
Tel: (604) 685 7337.
**The Salmon House on
the Hill ★★★**
Salmon is barbecued
over alderwood here, and
the view over the city is

spectacular.

2229 Folkstone Way.
Tel: (604) 926 3212.

Salt Tasting Room ★★★

Select local meat, cheese and wine.

45 Blood Alley, Gastown.
Tel: (604) 633 1912.

Transcontinental Restaurant ★★★

Classic surf and turf in the gorgeously remodelled CP Railway Terminus.

601 West Cordova St.
Tel: (604) 678 8000.

West ★★★★

Named the best restaurant in Vancouver, West takes French food and gives it a mouthwatering West Coast twist!

2881 Granville St.
Tel: (604) 738 8938.

Victoria

Camille's ★★★★

Good seasonal local food in the perfect spot for a romantic dinner.

45 Bastion Square.
Tel: (250) 381 3433.

J+J Wonton Noodle House ★★

A local favourite, the best noodles and fresh seafood.

1012 Fort St.
Tel: (250) 383 0680.

Millos ★★★

Look for a blue and white windmill downtown for great Greek food and entertainment.

716 Burdett Ave.
Tel: (250) 382 4422.

Sam's Deli ★

Popular soup and sandwich lunch spot across the street from the harbour.

805 Government St.
Tel: (250) 382 8424.

Sooke Harbour House ★★★

Spectacular views and a commitment to local ingredients.

1528 Whiffen Spit Rd, Sooke.
Tel: (250) 642 3421,
freephone (800) 889 9688.

Spinnaker's Brew Pub ★★

Great beers accompany average food in this informal pub.

308 Catherine St, Victoria West.
Tel: (250) 384 6613.

Il Terrazzo ★★★★

About as good as Northern Italian cuisine comes, with meals alfresco all year round by outdoor fireplaces if you choose.

555 Johnson St.
Tel: (250) 361 0028.

Pubs

There are few traditional British-style pubs in BC, probably because the province is too young, the population too transitory and the drinking laws too strict. Until the BC government first permitted neighbourhood pubs in the late 1960s, most public drinking was confined to hotels and restaurants. The pubs that do exist today include some good ones attached to local breweries. Good local brews, usually on tap, come from Steamworks Brewing, Yaletown Brewing Company, Granville Island Brewing and Whistler Brewing lagers. There was also Horseshoe Bay Brewing, which, when it opened in 1981, was the first cottage brewery built in Canada in 50 years. It closed down in 2000.

Generally speaking, the further the watering hole from the big city, the friendlier the staff and the clientele.

Fanny Bay Inn
This is one of the oldest pubs, built in 1938, and famous for its oysters, barbecued beef, pork and lamb, and staff who make visitors feel like locals.
4480 S Island Road, near Courtenay, Vancouver Island.
Tel: (250) 335 2323.
Kingston Taphouse & Grille
Contemporary urban pub and restaurant with six unique rooms in the heart of Vancouver.

755 Richards St.
Tel: (604) 681 7011.
The Lennox Pub
Celtic touches, an outdoor patio, extensive beer and single malt scotch offerings.
800 Granville St.
Tel: (604) 408 0881.
Moose's Down Under Restaurant
This Australian-style pub is open for breakfast, lunch and dinner, and offers exceptional value.
830 West Pender St.
Tel: (604) 683 3300.

Steamworks Brewing Company
A lovely old heritage building is the location of this pub, with good beer and home-made food.
375 Water St, Gastown.
Tel: (604) 689 2739.
Yaletown Brewing Company
Right in the heart of trendy Yaletown. Pizzas are made in a traditional wood oven.
1111 Mainland St.
Tel: (604) 681 BREW.

Food and drink

A tasting after the tour at Granville Island Brewing

Hotels and accommodation

Accommodation in BC ranges from rustic campsites to sybaritic suites with all amenities. Reservations are recommended, especially during the crowded days of summer. The Travel InfoCentre (HelloBC), at 200 Burrard Street, operates a hotel reservation service (tel: (604) 663 6000). Current hotel tax is 16 per cent, but hold on to your receipts as you may be eligible for a refund when you leave the country. HelloBC will provide free tourism information and the comprehensive BC Accommodations Guide.

De luxe hotels

Two of Canada's five-diamond CAA/AAA hotels are in Vancouver: the **Four Seasons** (*tel: (604) 689 9333; www.fourseasons.com*) and **Sutton Place** (*tel: (604) 682 5511; www.vancouver. suttonplace.com*). The Four Seasons sits atop the Pacific Centre's underground mall of 200 shops; Sutton Place also manages the spacious apartments in **La Grande Residence** next door (minimum stay one month).

Most luxury hotels have pools, spas, restaurants, 24-hour room service and valet parking, and most are wheelchair-accessible. Rates run from C$290 per room per night. De luxe downtown hotels include the **Fairmont Hotel Vancouver** (*tel: (604) 684 3131; www.fairmont.com*), a city landmark which has undergone a C$10 million renovation, and has a brand-new spa; the **Hyatt Regency** (*tel: (604) 683 1234; www.vancouver.hyatt.com*) above the Royal Centre Mall; the sparkling **Pan Pacific** (*tel: (604) 662 8111;*

www.panpac.com), overlooking the harbour; the **Renaissance** (*tel: (604) 689 9211; www.renaissancevancouver.com*), with its revolving restaurant; the **Westin Bayshore and Marina** (*tel: (604) 682 3377; www.westinbayshore.com*), Vancouver's only downtown resort hotel; and the **Fairmont Waterfront Centre Hotel** (*tel: (604) 691 1991; www.fairmont.com*) behind the Pan Pacific.

Moderately priced hotels

These hotels, priced from about C$140 for a double room, offer comfortable and clean accommodation.

Moderately priced hotels include the **Barclay Hotel** (*tel: (604) 688 8850; www.barclayhotel.com*), an 85-room European-style establishment with a licensed lounge and restaurant; the **Sandman Hotel** (*tel: (604) 681 2211, freephone (800) Sandman; www.sandmanhotels.com*), within walking distance of Robson Street, Chinatown and Gastown; the

Oceanside Apartment Hotel (*tel: (604) 682 5641, freephone (877) 506 2326; www.oceanside-hotel.com*), on English Bay, two blocks from Stanley Park; the **Riviera Hotel** (*tel: (604) 685 1301, freephone (888) 699 5222; www.vancouver-bc. com/rivierahotel*) on Robson St, which offers 40 suites with balconies; the **Sunset Inn** (*tel: (604) 688 2474, freephone (800) 786 1997; www.sunsetinn.com*), which has 50 suites with kitchens (weekly and monthly rates available); and the **Best Western Château** (*tel: (604) 669 7070, freephone (800) 663 7070; www.bwcg.com*), on Granville Street, mostly suite accommodation close to all downtown attractions. Also check out the **Rosellen Suites** at Stanley Park (*tel: (604) 689 4807, (888) 317 6648; www.rosellensuites.com*) and the **Victorian Hotel** (*tel: (604) 681 6369; fax: (604) 681 8776; www.victorianhotel.ca*).

Cost-cutters

Several reasonably priced hotels (from about C$75 for a double room) are found throughout the downtown area. **Shaughnessy Village** (*tel: (604) 736 5511; www.shaughnessyvillage.com*) rooms are small but the hotel has amenities galore: free health club, 24-hr movies, miniature golf and more. The **Kingston Hotel** (*tel: (604) 684 9024; www.kingstonhotelvancouver.com*) offers a complimentary breakfast and a 10 per cent discount for senior citizens and students. The **YMCA** (*tel: (604) 681 0221; www.vanymca.org*) offers good

bargains for single people and couples. **Pillow Suites** (*tel: (604) 879 8977; www.pillow.net*) offer homely and neat suites with fully equipped kitchens.

The **Vancouver Youth Hostel** (*tel: (604) 684 4565; www.hihostels.bc.ca*) is located in Vancouver's lively West End within minutes of shops, restaurants and beaches. Heaps of amenities.

The **University of British Columbia** (*tel: (604) 822 1000; www. pacificspirithostel.com*) and **Simon Fraser University** (*tel: (604) 291 4503; www.sfu.ca/conference-accommodation*) offer summer housing from May through to August. Both have single rooms with shared bath, and UBC also has several studio and one-bed suites.

Bed-and-breakfast

Greater Vancouver has numerous bed-and-breakfast establishments. When booking, enquire whether smoking is permitted and credit cards are accepted. To find a B&B, check Western Canada Bed & Breakfast Innkeepers Association (*www.wcbbia.com*) or call HelloBC (*tel: (604) 663 6000*).

Campsites

Several campsites are scattered throughout the city, but the **Capilano RV Park** (*tel: (604) 987 4722; fax: (604) 987 2015; www.capilanorvpark.com*) in North Vancouver has the most dramatic setting. There are sites for 190 motorhomes and 10 tents. The park has 24-hour-a-day supervision, a TV lounge, a Jacuzzi and a swimming pool.

Practical guide

Arriving

Entry formalities

Requirements include a valid full passport (except for Americans) and a return or onward ticket, together with evidence of sufficient funds for the duration of your stay. Visas are not required for citizens of Britain, Ireland, Australia, New Zealand and the USA. Visitors under 18 years of age unaccompanied by an adult must carry a letter from a parent or guardian granting permission to travel in Canada.

Visitors are only allowed to work in Canada if authorisation was obtained prior to entry into the country.

Numerous international airlines serve Vancouver with regularly scheduled flights from Europe, Asia, the South Pacific, the USA, Mexico and South America. Vancouver International Airport and Canada Customs and Immigration can be very busy in summer and at Christmas and Easter.

Customs (*tel: (604) 666 0545*) and immigration (*www.cic.gc.ca*) regulations are strict, and baggage may be searched. Fruit and animal products may not be imported. There is no inbound duty-free shop.

Vancouver Airport is a 30-minute drive from downtown. Taxis from Level II (Domestic Arrivals) cost about C\$20–30 to go downtown. Airporter buses (*tel: (604) 946 8866, freephone (800) 668 3141; www.yvrairporter.com*) also leave from Level II every 20 minutes and stop at major downtown hotels and the Greyhound Bus Depot. The cost is about C\$14 one way or C\$21 round-trip per person. Passengers en route to Whistler can take the direct Perimeter's Whistler Express bus (*tel: (604) 266 5386; www.perimeterbus.com*), and there are also direct buses to the BC Ferries terminal where you can connect to Victoria or Nanaimo on Vancouver Island.

Camping

Camping is a wonderful way to enjoy the fresh air and natural beauty and to make new friends, especially in summer. There are hundreds of campsites in BC, several of them in Greater Vancouver. The Capilano RV Campground (*tel: (604) 987 4722*), a ten-minute drive across the Lions Gate Bridge from the city centre, is one of the best urban camping areas in the world. Suburban campsites include the Burnaby Cariboo RV Park (*tel: (604) 420 1722, global freephone fax: (0800) 408 55470; www.bcrv.com*) and Richmond RV Park (*tel: (604) 270 7878; www.welcometobc.ca/vancamping/*). Peace Arch RV Park (*tel: (604) 594 7009; www.peacearchrvpark.com*) and Plaza RV Park (*tel: (604) 594 4440*) are in Surrey. The campsite at Porteau Cove Provincial Park (*tel: (604) 986 9371*) overlooks Howe Sound, the most southerly fiord in North America. For an extensive listing of BC campsites, visit *www.env.gov.bc.ca/bcparks*

Mountain Equipment Co-op (130 W Broadway; *tel: (604) 872 7858; www.mec.ca*) hires tents, camping equipment and other sporting goods.

For more information, pick up the *SuperCamping* booklet from any Travel InfoCentre, which lists private campsites, BC parks and RV and motorhome dealers.

Children

Vancouver is a great place for a family holiday (*see pp154–5*). Children love the spacious parks and playgrounds to romp and roam. Public transport, whether on planes, trains, buses or ferries, offers reduced fares for young-sters, who particularly enjoy roaming around the decks of the big BC ferries. Most Vancouver attractions offer reduced admission prices for children.

Many hotels make an extra effort to cater to children, with special menus, reduced room rates and other services. The Westin Grand (*tel: (604) 602 1999*) has a Kids Club that includes welcome gifts, entertainment options and easy access to loaner strollers, high chairs and other useful amenities.

For a list of special treats for kids, check *www.kidsvancouver.com* that lists year-round and rainy-day things to do such as the Granville Island Museums (*tel: (604) 683 1939*) with their huge display of toy and model trains or

special current events for kids. The Vancouver TouristInfo Centre also has its comprehensive *Kids' Guide to Vancouver*, and *Kids friendly! British Columbia* (*tel: (604) 541 6192; www.kidfriendly.org*) directs visitors to business and enterprises that are decidedly 'kid friendly.' HelloBC (*tel: freephone (800) 435 5622; www. hellobc.com*) is another good contact for rooting out children's activities.

In addition to museums, parks, aquatic centres and special indoor play areas, the city and neighbouring communities have a host of special events through the year including the Vancouver International Children's Festival each May. Playland, open from Easter throughout the summer, offers various historic sites and many splashdown parks and water slides. The Cloverdale Rodeo each Victoria Day is a huge attraction.

Climate

Compared with other cities in Canada, Vancouver and Victoria have a moderate climate, thanks in part to Pacific Ocean currents. There are few extremes in temperature. Vancouver's highest recorded temperature is 33°C (91°F) and the lowest is −18°C (0°F). But clouds and rain can be abundant, especially during the winter months of November, December and January. While about 100cm (39in) of rain fall on Vancouver Airport each year, some areas of the North Shore receive as much as 250cm (98in) annually. As a rule, the summer months of June, July and August are the driest and sunniest. Monthly hours of sunshine average 305 in July and 44 in December. For a recorded weather report, call Environment Canada (*tel: (604) 664 9010*), which also predicts the possibility of rain.

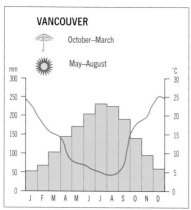

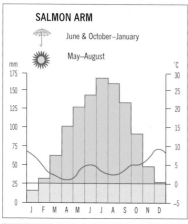

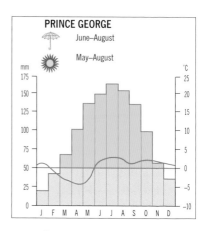

WEATHER CONVERSION CHART

25.4mm = 1 inch
°F = 1.8 × °C + 32

Consulates

Embassies are located in Ottawa, Canada's capital, but among the consulates in Vancouver are the following:

Australia: *888 Dunsmuir Street. Tel: (604) 684 1177.*
New Zealand: *888 Dunsmuir Street. Tel: (604) 684 7388.*
UK: *1111 Melville Street. Tel: (604) 683 4421.*
United States: *1075 West Pender Street. Tel: (604) 685 4311.*

Crime

Vancouver is still a generally safe city, compared with such vast urban centres as London and New York. Downtown streets are well lit, but caution and common sense are good watchwords. Report any theft immediately to your hotel and the police.

Customs regulations

Duty-free allowances for visitors aged 19 and older are 200 cigarettes or 50 cigars or 1kg of tobacco, 1.14 litres of spirits or wine or 24 cans or bottles of beer or ale, and other dutiable goods up to a limit of C$200 in value. There is no duty on personal belongings for use during your visit. Gifts valued at more than C$60 are subject to duty and tax on the excess amount. Any currency carried worth C$10,000 or more must be declared. Revolvers, pistols and fully automatic firearms are prohibited entry into Canada. Quarantine regulations are strict. Plants must be declared and inspected by Agriculture Canada; animals may be quarantined for up to three months. The Customs website *www.cbsa-asfc.gc.ca* provides full information.

Driving
Breakdowns

The BC Automobile Association (*tel: (604) 293 2222*) honours memberships of other automobile associations around the world. Any automobile club card is also valid for discounts at various hotels and attractions. Request the CAA discount when making reservations. For information on highway conditions, available for free, contact the *Talking Yellow Pages* (*Vancouver tel: (604) 299 6581 greater Vancouver area, (250) 861 2929 rest of BC; on Telus mobility, call *4997*). The service is available in most cities and towns in Canada. On the BC Highways website, webcam images show a continually updated image of highway conditions: *www.th.gov.bc.ca/ bchighwaycam*

Practical guide

CONVERSION TABLE

FROM	TO	MULTIPLY BY
Inches	Centimetres	2.54
Feet	Metres	0.3048
Yards	Metres	0.9144
Miles	Kilometres	1.6090
Acres	Hectares	0.4047
Gallons	Litres	4.5460
Ounces	Grams	28.35
Pounds	Grams	453.6
Pounds	Kilograms	0.4536
Tons	Tonnes	1.0160

To convert back, for example from centimetres to inches, divide by the number in the third column.

MEN'S SUITS

UK	36	38	40	42	44	46	48
Rest of Europe	46	48	50	52	54	56	58
USA	36	38	40	42	44	46	48

DRESS SIZES

UK	8	10	12	14	16	18
France	36	38	40	42	44	46
Italy	38	40	42	44	46	48
Rest of Europe	34	36	38	40	42	44
USA	6	8	10	12	14	16

MEN'S SHIRTS

UK	14	14.5	15	15.5	16	16.5	17
Rest of Europe	36	37	38	39/40	41	42	43
USA	14	14.5	15	15.5	16	16.5	17

MEN'S SHOES

UK	7	7.5	8.5	9.5	10.5	11
Rest of Europe	41	42	43	44	45	46
USA	8	8.5	9.5	10.5	11.5	12

WOMEN'S SHOES

UK	4.5	5	5.5	6	6.5	7
Rest of Europe	38	38	39	39	40	41
USA	6	6.5	7	7.5	8	8.5

Car hire

Hiring a car is relatively inexpensive. Vehicles may be hired through Thomas Cook branches (*see p183*). Major car hire (rental) companies include:

Avis (*tel: (604) 606 2866*);
Budget (*tel: (604) 668 7000*);
Hertz (*tel: (604) 606 3782*);
National Car Rental
(*tel: (604) 207 3730*).

A major credit card is required to hire a car (otherwise a passport, a return ticket and a cash deposit), even if you plan to pay cash. The VISA Gold Card, among others, provides free car insurance; if you are planning to hire a car for a few weeks, it is worth investing in a gold credit card if you qualify. The minimum age to hire a car is 21.

The companies listed also hire campervans, motorhomes and four-wheel-drive vehicles. Chauffeured limousines and other vehicles are also available. For the budget-minded, try **Rent-A-Wreck** (*tel: (604) 688 0001*). Car-hire companies can charge double to fill up the tank, so it is better to do it yourself before returning the car. Remember to drive on the right in Canada.

Petrol

Petrol (gas) is sold by the litre in regular, premium or super grades, all unleaded, and is reasonably priced.

Electricity

Canada's electric current is an alternating 110–120 volts and 60 cycles. Adaptors are sold in some hotel shops and at Gulliver's Travels in Park Royal (*tel: (604) 922 9650*) and the Sinclair shopping centres.

Emergency telephone numbers

Ambulance: *911* or *0* for operator.
Dental service: contact your hotel concierge for a recommendation.
Emotional Crisis Centre: *(604) 872 3311.*
Fire and rescue: *911* or *0* for operator.
Marine and Aircraft distress: *(800) 567 5111.*
MasterCard: *1 800 307 7309* (freephone) for loss or theft of cards.
Poison Control Centre: *(604) 682 5050.*
Police: *911* or *0* for operator.
Prescription Service: contact your hotel concierge; prescriptions are available only by visiting a Canadian doctor.
RCMP Freeway Patrol: *911* or *0* for operator.
Thomas Cook traveller's cheque loss or theft: call *00 44 1733 318950* (*freephone*) to report lost or stolen cheques within 24 hours (*see also* Money matters, *pp182–3*).

Health

No vaccinations are required for entry into Canada.

Tap water is usually safe to drink. Campers are advised to boil water from lakes and rivers. Canadian health-care standards are high. If you become ill, ask your hotel to recommend a nearby doctor.

Medical insurance, which should cover the duration of your stay in Canada is essential, as medical services are expensive. A visit to a general practitioner, or a stay in a hospital, could be a costly affair.

Hire facilities
Bicycles
Cycling around Stanley Park and other areas of Vancouver is a wonderful way to explore the city and enjoy the sights. Contact Spokes Bicycle Rentals (*tel: (604) 688 5141*) at the Georgia Street entrance to the park, or check the *Yellow Pages* of the telephone directory.

Boats
Sailing boats, motorboats and houseboats are available for hire from dozens of companies both in and outside Vancouver.

Contact the nearest Travel InfoCentre for details.

Hitchhiking
Hitchhiking is not illegal, indeed many backpackers do it, but it is not a recommended form of travel.

Insurance
Any medical, baggage or other personal insurance should be purchased before leaving home.

Any vehicle hire automatically includes third-party-liability insurance for damage to people and property.

Loss and damage insurance, which covers the hire car, costs extra, as do personal accident insurance and personal effects coverage for the driver and passengers.

Language
Canada has two official languages: English and French. English is the predominant language of BC. However, thanks to the native Indians and continuing waves of immigrants from Europe, Asia and around the world, many other languages, ranging from Chinook to Vietnamese, are also spoken. Canadian English has been most influenced by Americans, primarily through the media and advertising. Following are a few words familiar to British Columbians, but foreign to many visitors:

Anglophone English-speaking person
bannock Indian bread
bar a ridge of sand or gravel in a stream or river where gold may be found by panning, but also a drinking place
First Nations native Indian people
Inuit Eskimo
Mountie RCMP officer
potlatch a native Indian festival
saltchuk ocean

Lost property
Vancouver has two lost property centres: BC Transit (bus, SkyTrain losses) *tel: (604) 682 7887*, and Police (lost property rooms). Otherwise check with the nearest police station or call the head office of BC Transit.

Maps

Maps of Vancouver and BC are available from any Travel InfoCentre.

Media

Newspapers and magazines

The best daily in the country, the morning *Globe & Mail*, has limited local news. However, *The Province* (*www.vancouverprovince.com*), a tabloid, and *The Vancouver Sun* (*www.vancouversun.com*), a broadsheet, both morning papers, cover city news and events. *The Georgia Strait* covers the Vancouver arts and entertainment scene. All three are available at news-stands and in street coin boxes. The weekly *Westender,* published on Thursdays, provides compact coverage of entertainment and other downtown and West End events, and is available free at most hotels. The monthly *WHERE Vancouver* is also available in hotels at no charge and for a dollar in coin boxes at the SeaBus Terminal. It is designed especially for visitors and includes information on shopping, dining, attractions, entertainment, special events, maps and evening television programmes.

For general information on what's on in Vancouver, visit the website *www.allianceforarts.com* (*hotline: (604) 684 2787*), *www.mybc.com,* or *www.showtimetickets.com* (*tel: (604) 688 5000 or freephone (800) 480-SHOW*), an online ticket reservation service for concert or theatre events.

The Tourism Vancouver tourist information centre is at *Waterfront Centre, 200 Burrard Street* (*tel: (604) 682 2222; www.tourismvancouver.com*). Tourism BC (*tel: freephone 1 800 HELLO BC; www.hellobc.com*).

Radio and television

Favourite local radio stations include CBC at 690 AM and CKNW 980 (talk, music and sport); CHQM at 1320 AM (memory music); and 103.5 FM (contemporary music).

Local television stations include CBC-TV (Canadian Broadcasting Corporation) on Cable 3; BCTV (the CTV network) on Cable 11; and the Knowledge Network (the BC educational channel) on Cable 5 (no commercials). Dozens of other channels, including PBS, ABC, CBS and NBC from the USA, are also available locally. Check the listings at the back of *WHERE Vancouver* magazine.

Money matters

Currency

Canada has a decimal currency system with 100 cents to the dollar. Coins are one cent, five cents (a nickel), 10 cents (a dime), 25 cents (a quarter) and the one-dollar coin called a 'loonie' (because of the loon bird on one face). The bills (notes) are colour-coded: $5 is blue, $10 is purple, $20 is green, $50 is red, $100 is beige; $2 is now a coin called the 'twoonie'. Merchants seem reluctant to give up a lot of change, so $100-bills are not popular, while $20-bills are always acceptable. Thomas Cook traveller's cheques in Canadian or

US dollars are a secure and convenient way of carrying larger amounts of money and can be used as cash in most hotels and restaurants.

Money exchange

Most foreign currencies and traveller's cheques can be exchanged at the foreign exchange counters at the airport, at all major city banks and at some hotels.

Since exchange rates fluctuate, check the Canadian dollar rates on your arrival in Canada. Credit cards, such as American Express, MasterCard and VISA, are widely accepted. ATMs will accept debit cards, however check the charges before using them as they may be very expensive.

If you need to transfer money quickly, you can use the MoneyGram^{SM} Money transfer service. For more details, call freephone *0800 897198* (in the UK).

Taxes

The federal GST (Goods and Services Tax) is currently 7 per cent. However, foreign visitors may claim a rebate when purchases total more than C$100. Pick up a rebate form at the nearest Travel InfoCentre, or call freephone *1 800 668 4748* for further details. BC provincial sales tax (exempt from children's clothing and food) is 7 per cent on most merchandise, BC hotels charge an 8 per cent tax, plus the 7 per cent GST, and 10 per cent is added to the price of liquor consumed in bars and restaurants.

National holidays

Banks, post offices, liquor stores, government offices, most other offices and many shops are closed on these holidays. City buses, the SeaBus and the SkyTrain operate on a reduced schedule. Vancouver hotels are rarely fully booked during Canadian holidays, but there are seldom rooms available during American holidays.

New Year's Day 1 January
Good Friday late March, early April
Easter late March, early April
Victoria Day 24 May or the preceding Monday
Canada Day 1 July
BC Day 1 August
Labour Day first Monday in September
Thanksgiving Day second Monday in October
Remembrance Day 11 November
Christmas Day 25 December
Boxing Day 26 December

Opening times

Banks Major banks downtown open at 8am. Some banks are open on Saturday morning, but all are closed on Sundays and holidays. Normal banking hours are 10am–4pm Monday to Friday, often extending to 5pm on Friday.
Museums, galleries and attractions Most are open daily 10am–5pm, but some are closed one day a week, and some have extended or shortened hours on certain days.

Post offices All post offices are open Monday to Friday 8.30am–5.30pm. Some sub-offices are open Saturday mornings, and postal counters in 7-Eleven stores are open until 11pm.

Shops Most shops and stores are open Monday to Friday 9.30am–6pm, with hours extended to 9pm on Thursday and Friday. Most are open Saturday 9.30am–5.30pm, and many are open on Sunday, noon–5pm. Such convenience stores as 7-Eleven are often open 7am–11pm, and some are open all night.

Pharmacies

Medical prescriptions in BC are available only through a local doctor. Many pharmacies are hidden at the back of big drugstores (chemists). These sell all kinds of non-prescription medicines, along with contraceptives, insect repellent, vitamins, tissues and a host of other items. Shoppers Drug Mart, at *1125 Davie Street* (*tel: (604) 669 2424*), is open 24 hours a day, seven days a week. London Drugs, at *1187 Robson Street* (*tel: (604) 448 4819*), is open from Monday to Saturday 9am–11pm and on Sunday 10am–10pm.

Photography

Print film can be developed within an hour or two at numerous photo shops. Slide film, sold primarily in photo shops, takes 24 hours to develop, except for Kodachrome, which takes a week. Lens & Shutter, at *700 Dunsmuir Street* (*tel: (604) 684 4422*), provides a reliable

service for both prints and slides. Many shops sell disposable cameras and supplies for digital cameras.

Copy shops and internet cafés are good places to burn your photos to CD. Try Webster's Internet Café at 300 Robson Street (*tel: (604) 915 9327*).

Places of worship

Places of worship representing various denominations and faiths in and around Vancouver include:

Akali Singh Sikh Temple
1890 Skeena St.
Tel: (604) 254 2117.
Beth Israel Synagogue
4350 Oak St. Tel: (604) 731 4161.
Canadian Memorial United Church
1825 W 16th Ave. Tel: (604) 731 3101.
Central Presbyterian Church
1155 Thurlow St. Tel: (604) 683 1913.
Christ Church Anglican Cathedral
690 Burrard St. Tel: (604) 682 3848.
Christian Science Church
1900 W 12th Ave. Tel: (604) 733 8040.
First Baptist Church
969 Burrard St. Tel: (604) 683 8441.
Holy Rosary Catholic Cathedral
646 Richards St. Tel: (604) 682 6774.
Ismaili Mosque
4010 Canada Way, Burnaby.
Tel: (604) 438 4010.

Police

The RCMP (Royal Canadian Mounted Police) cover areas where there is no municipal police force. Call *911* or *0* for the operator for any emergencies.

Post offices

The main post office at 349 West Georgia Street is open from Monday to Friday 8.30am–5.30pm. Many sub-offices in malls, drugstores, convenience stores and even dry-cleaning shops are also open on Saturday as well. Most offer postage, courier and facsimile (fax) services. Canada Post boxes are red. Mail can be received 'c/o General Delivery' at any post office in Canada. To send a telegram, contact Canada Post.

Senior citizens

Numerous transport and tour companies, hotels, shops, attractions and events offer reduced rates to people as young as 50. Carry an ID card or any other official document that indicates your birth date.

The Hyatt, Park Royal and Westin Bayshore hotels, among others, offer senior discounts. Many local restaurants give 10 to 20 per cent discount to seniors, while others offer small-portion meals and early-bird specials – enquire upon entering any restaurant.

Domestic airlines, the harbour and Granville Island ferries, city transport including the SeaBus and SkyTrain all offer reduced fares to seniors. Call the company directly for details. Such attractions as the Vancouver Aquarium, the Dr Sun Yat-Sen Chinese Garden, the Vancouver Art Gallery, the Museum of Anthropology, the Maritime Museum, Science World, the IMAX show, the Bloedel Conservatory and Grouse Mountain offer reduced admission prices to seniors. The Vancouver Aquatic Centre offers a seniors' programme which includes exercises on the deck and in the pool, and organises day trips outside the city, and such special events as Valentine Tea.

City cinemas, theatres and the symphony offer reduced rates to seniors, sometimes by as much as

Christ Church Cathedral with the Hotel Vancouver in the background

50 per cent. Some supermarkets, chemists and department stores reduce prices by 10 to 15 per cent one day a month for seniors.

Travel-wise seniors get great holiday bargains through Elderhostel at *33 Prince Arthur Avenue, Toronto, Ontario M5R 1B2.* A monthly publication, *The Independent Times* (*tel: (604) 580 1844*), is geared to the needs of senior readers and can be found at Shoppers Drug Mart or some banks and travel information centres in season.

Student and youth travel

Many attractions and events in the Vancouver area offer reduced rates for students. Bring your student card.

Sustainable tourism

Thomas Cook is a strong advocate of ethical and fairly traded tourism and believes that the travel experience should be as good for the places visited as it is for the people who visit them. That's why we firmly support The Travel Foundation, a charity that develops solutions to help improve and protect holiday destinations, their environment, traditions and culture. To find out what you can do to make a positive difference to the places you travel to and the people who live there, please visit *www.thetravelfoundation.org.uk*

Telephones

Public telephones can be found in post offices, hotel lobbies, public buildings, and in phone booths on various streets throughout the city. Local calls cost 25 cents for an unlimited time. Some public phones are specifically for long-distance calls and some are designated for credit card use only. Both local and international calls are usually more expensive on hotel phones. Inexpensive long-distance phonecards are available under a variety of names and can be purchased at post offices and a variety of other stores. Call *0* for the operator to enquire about discounts for dialling both domestically and abroad at certain times. The area codes for BC are *604* for the lower mainland to Hope and north to Whistler, and *250* for the rest of the province.

International calls can be dialled direct using the following codes: Britain is *011 +44* + city code minus the initial *0* + number, Australia *011 +61* + city code + number, and New Zealand *011 +64* + city code + number. For calls to other provinces of Canada and to the USA, dial *1*, the area code and the number.

Ticket agencies

For such events as opera, symphony, ballet, theatre, sports, rock concerts and some attractions, call Ticketmaster on *(604) 280 4444.* By telephone you can pay by American Express, MasterCard or VISA, while at counters scattered throughout city shopping malls, you can pay either by credit card or cash. Cinema tickets are, however, sold only at individual theatres. For programme times at Cineplex Odeon, you should check *www.cineplex.com*

Time

Most of BC is on Pacific Standard Time, which in summer is nine hours behind GMT. Clocks are put back an hour on the last Sunday in October, and an hour forward on the first Sunday in April, for daylight-saving time. Vancouver time is the same as California, three hours behind Toronto and New York. For most of the year, Vancouver is 18 hours behind Sydney and 21 hours behind Auckland.

Tipping

Tips generally range from 10 to 20 per cent in restaurants and bars, and for taxis. Tipping is optional for porters, doormen, chambermaids and other service personnel.

Toilets

Public toilets are found in railway and bus terminals, shopping centres and department stores. A hotel or restaurant will sometimes let you use its facilities.

Tourist offices

For maps and brochures on Vancouver and BC, contact:
Tourism BC *PO Box 9830, 1 Stn. A, Prov. Govt., Victoria BC V8W 9W5. Tel: (800) HelloBC freephone; or (604) HelloBC; www.hellobc.com*

Tours

UK-based travellers can pre-book a range of tours and travel options at advantageous rates when arranging their trip with Thomas Cook Holidays (details from any branch of Thomas Cook, or if in the UK by telephoning *01733 417000*). Visitors to Vancouver can take to the water aboard the SeaBus or the Granville Island and BC ferries, in a canoe or kayak, or on a motorboat or yacht. Landlubbers can tour on foot and by bicycle, antique car, bus, train or limousine. Some visitors take to the air in seaplanes, gliders, helicopters and hot-air balloons. Although North American travellers tend to be do-it-yourself sightseers or rely on friends and relatives, numerous commercial tours are available, especially in summer. Many can be pre-booked within your overall travel plan. The booklet *Official Visitors' Guide*, stocked at Travel InfoCentres, is helpful (and can also be requested through *www.tourismvancouver.com* or *www.hellobc.com*).

Bicycle tours

Cycling BC (*332–1367 West Broadway. Tel: (604) 737 3034; www.cycling.bc.ca*) is the umbrella organisation for several cycling clubs, including the Vancouver Bike Club which welcomes non-members to join in city cycling and tours further afield.

Bus and car tours

Gray Line (*tel: (800) 667 0882*) and Pacific Coach Lines (*tel: (604) 662 7575*) among others, offer various sightseeing tours, with itineraries ranging from a city circle, similar to the Trolley tour (*see pp36–7*), and an evening dinner tour (a great way to meet fellow travellers), to a seven-day return ride through the Rockies to Calgary. Early Motion Tours (*tel: (604) 687 5088*) offer the luxury of a finely tuned original 1928 or 1930 Model A Ford Phaeton convertible. The driver, former teacher called 'Fridge' Fridulin, provides a continuous commentary on city sights and a Polaroid photograph of you and the Phaeton as a souvenir. Limojet Gold (*tel: (604) 273 1331; freephone (800) 278 8742; www.limojetgold.com*) creates tailored tours in the luxury of a limousine, day or night, in addition to airport and intercity transfer.

Historical walking tours

Local historian Chuck Davis (*tel: (604) 583 2920*), who probably knows Vancouver past and present better than anyone, designs walking tours of the city centre to meet your requirements.

Water tours

Gray Line (*tel: (800) 667 0882*) and the SS *Beaver* (*tel: N113040 on Van 25; marine radio via the 'O' operator*) offer harbour sightseeing excursions. Harbour Cruises offers a four-hour tour of Indian Arm (*tel: (604) 688 7246*). Both Gray Line and Bayshore Yacht Charters (*tel: (604) 691 6936*), offer three-hour dinner cruises. Sewell's Landing Marina (*tel: (604) 921 3474*) in Horseshoe Bay offers skippered fishing tours. For white-water

rafting from May to September, contact Hyak Wilderness Adventures (*tel: (604) 734 8622*). The company's shuttle service runs from Vancouver to the Chilliwack, Thompson and Chilko rivers.

Transport
Airlines

Air BC & Air Canada (*tel: 1 888 247 2262; www.aircanada.com*)
Harbour Air (*tel: (604) 274 1277; freephone (800) 665; www.harbour-air.com*)
Helijet Airways (*tel: (604) 273 4688; www.helijet.com*)
West Jet Airlines (*tel: 1 888 WEST JET; www.westjet.com*)

Buses

Airport Express (*tel: (604) 946 8866; www.yvrairporter.com*) operates between the airport and downtown.
Gray Line (*tel: (800) 667 0882; www.graylinewest.com*) offers sightseeing tours.
Greyhound (*tel: (800) 661 8747; www.greyhound.ca*) operates throughout Canada.
Traxx Coachlines (*tel: (604) 255 1171; www.traxxcoachlines.com*) runs to Whistler.
BC Transit (*tel: (604) 453 4500; www.bctransit.com*), Vancouver's regional public transport system, includes buses, the SeaBus and the SkyTrain, which run along major arteries through the city centre and suburbs. There are three fare zones in

Greater Vancouver. Day passes are available for children, adults and senior citizens. Exact change in coins is preferred, but tickets and passes are sold at 7-Eleven and other stores.

Transit timetables are available from public libraries, city and municipal halls, Travel InfoCentres and BC Transit offices and terminals. For Blue Bus routes and schedules from downtown to West Vancouver, call *(604) 985 7777*.

The SeaBuses, which are actually 400-passenger catamaran ferries, make the 15-minute trip across Burrard Inlet to North Vancouver every 15 minutes. The SkyTrain (*tel: (604) 520 3641*) runs 28km (17½ miles) from Canada Place downtown to King George Station, beyond New Westminster, with 15 stops en route. Trains run every 3–5 minutes at an average speed of 75km per hour (47 mph).

Ferries

The little Aquabus Ferries operating from the foot of Hornby Street, and the False Creek ferries from the Aquatic Centre, make the five-minute run to and from Granville Island all year round. BC Ferries (*tel: 1 888 223 3779*) carry both vehicles and foot passengers and run from Tsawwassen (an hour's drive south from the city centre) to Swartz Bay (a half-hour from Victoria) and Nanaimo on Vancouver Island, and to the Gulf Islands. From Horseshoe Bay (a half-hour drive northwest from downtown Vancouver), ferries sail to Nanaimo, Bowen Island and the Sunshine Coast.

Taxis

It is hard to hail a cab in downtown Vancouver – head to the nearest big hotel, where taxis usually wait in line, or call one of the following:
Black Top (*tel: (604) 731 1111*).
Yellow Cab (*tel: (604) 681 1111 or (604) 876 5555*).

Trains

VIA Rail (*tel: (888) 842 7245; www.viarail.ca*) operates a thrice-weekly passenger service across Canada, departing from the station on Main Street opposite Science World. VIA Rail's trans-Canadian train, the *Silver and Blue*, runs from Toronto to Vancouver and can be booked outside Canada. So can privately run Rocky Mountaineer Vacations, running from Vancouver through Jasper and Banff to Calgary.

Summer tours with Rocky Mountaineer Vacations (*tel: (604) 606 7245; www.rockymountaineer.com*) from Vancouver to Banff and Jasper are especially popular. Details of local rail, bus and ferry services are shown in the *Thomas Cook Overseas Timetable*, which is available to buy online from *www.thomascookpublishing.com*, from Thomas Cook branches in the UK or by phoning *01733 416477*.

Travellers with disabilities

For information on facilities for people with disabilities, contact any Travel InfoCentre, or the Canadian Paraplegic Association, at 780 Southwest Marine Drive, BC V6P 5Y7 (*tel: (604) 324 3611*).

190

Index

Acknowledgements

Thomas Cook Publishing wishes to thank HELENA ZUKOWSKI for the photographs reproduced in this book, to whom the copyright belongs, with the exception of the following:

CHIEN-HSIN KUO/VANCOUVER CIVIC THEATRES 65
MILLIE WAN/INTERNATIONAL BUDDHIST SOCIETY 67
LADY ROSE MARINE SERVICES 118, 119
CHRIS POTTER 121
DAVID BLUE/BARD ON THE BEACH 151
RICHARD SHAPKA 51, 91, 110
ROY STEWART 57, 82
MUSEUM OF ANTHROPOLOGY/BILL MCLENNAN 38 (The Raven and the First Men by Bill Reid, 1980), 59
VANCOUVER AQUARIUM/DIANE MORRISON 73a
GROUSE MOUNTAIN RESORT 79, 159
JEFF VINNICK/VANCOUVER CANUCKS 163
PAM MANDEL 1, 18, 87, 141, 165
WORLD PICTURES/PHOTOSHOT 39, 52, 53, 69, 109, 123, 135, 166
KAREN BEAULAH 45
WIKIMEDIA COMMONS 84 (Jeff Yang); 85, 185 (Thomas Quine); 101 (Tawker); 117 (Clayoquot); 146, 147, 149 (Arnold C); 167; 171 (Klauskk); 173 (Kingnothing83)
PICTURES COLOUR LIBRARY 145

Indexer: MARIE LORIMER

For CAMBRIDGE PUBLISHING MANAGEMENT LTD:
Project editor: Karen Beaulah
Typesetter: Julie Crane
Proofreader: Penny Isaac

SEND YOUR THOUGHTS TO
BOOKS@THOMASCOOK.COM

We're committed to providing the very best up-to-date information in our travel guides and constantly strive to make them as useful as they can be. You can help us to improve future editions by letting us have your feedback. If you've made a wonderful discovery on your travels that we don't already feature, if you'd like to inform us about recent changes to anything that we do include, or if you simply want to let us know your thoughts about this guidebook and how we can make it even better – we'd love to hear from you.

Send us ideas, discoveries and recommendations today and then look out for your valuable input in the next edition of this title.

Emails to the above address, or letters to Travellers Series Editor, Thomas Cook Publishing, PO Box 227, Coningsby Road, Peterborough PE3 8SB, UK.

Please don't forget to let us know which title your feedback refers to!